Unforgettable

WORDS OF PRAISE

"Phil Mershon is the master of creating memorable experiences. *Unforgettable* shares the secret recipe to turning a mundane event into a moment that can last a lifetime. This is the future of business and the blueprint of what it takes to stand out in today's noisy world."

—**Jesse Cole,** owner of the Savannah Bananas

"Anyone can host an event, but only the greats know how to create a memorable experience. In *Unforgettable*, Phil Mershon generously shares everything you need to know about how to create experiences that change how people feel, think, and act. This is the book we've been waiting for. Highly recommended."

—**Michael Port,** *New York Times* bestselling author of *Steal the Show*

"There is no quicker way to deepen relationships with customers or our team than creating an unforgettable event for them. All the more reason to get it right! Phil has systematized, categorized, and simplified the ultimate recipe for memorable events. Whether it's a live Zoom conference, a small retreat for your team, running a large conference, or even throwing your next birthday party, *Unforgettable* needs to be at the top of your list."

—**Chalene Johnson,** *New York Times* bestselling author of *Push*
and host of *The Chalene Show*

"I love creating unexpected, magical moments at the events I create. But to be honest, I've never had a recipe or a formula for doing that. It's mostly instinct and art. Finally, Phil Mershon—in his book *Unforgettable*—has provided a way to create that recipe for me and thousands of event organizers and creators. Now my team can create unforgettable experiences whether I'm there or not. So can you!"

—**JJ Virgin,** *New York Times* bestselling author of *The Virgin Diet*,
Founder, Mindshare Summit

"A great event deepens relationships, fast-forwards education, and creates a ripple effect that generates positive change for years to come. How do you create one? Read Phil's book. It's a map, it's a manifesto, it's a master plan for unforgettable events."

—**Jon Acuff,** *New York Times* bestselling author of
Soundtracks, the Surprising Solution to Overthinking

"Of the more than 1,000 events I've attended, I remember those planned by Phil Mershon the most. Do not plan an event without reading this brilliant book!"

—**Jay Baer,** Hall of Fame keynote speaker and coauthor of *Talk Triggers*

"Phil teaches how to create unforgettable events resulting in powerful memories for guests and for the team."

—**Lee Richter,** CEO & founder Global Leaders Collective

"If your event doesn't leave people with a profound experience, it's just a gathering. Sadly, most events are little more than gatherings with forgettable content, tedious schedules, and lukewarm buffets. You don't want that legacy. Event expert Phil Mershon has written *Unforgettable*—the definitive guide! Bring your highlighter and notepad. Delight your attendees by following the teachings within."

—**Joel Comm,** *New York Times* bestselling author of *The AdSense Code*
and International Keynote Speaker

"I know from experience, Phil Mershon practices what he preaches: exactly how to create an amazing experience. Combining customer service with a keen eye for details, Phil produces events that get attendees and speakers saying, "I'll be back!" If you want to create memorable events, read *Unforgettable*. Learn from a master."

—**Shep Hyken,** customer experience expert and
New York Times bestselling author of *The Amazement Revolution.*

"If I get to heaven and the Lord calls a meeting, training, or seminar, I'm in the other place. After reading this book, I've changed my mind—if the planners have read *Unforgettable*. You'll thank me for telling you about this book and Mershon for writing it."

—**Dr. Steve Brown,** founder, Key Life Network,
author, professor, broadcaster

"There is only one thing marketers agree on: You must be different. Stand out. When it comes to events, Phil Mershon is the wizard. Consider this book your go-to guide for events success!"

—**Mark Schaefer,** author of *Marketing Rebellion*

"Walt Disney understood more than anyone the power of *experiences*. Phil does a remarkable job of giving us tangible tips we can use to turn our events into immersive and *Unforgettable* experiences!"

—**Duncan Wardle,** founder iD8 Studios

"*Unforgettable* is a blueprint on how to pay fanatical attention to the details and build a lasting experience in your industry or outside. Mershon's magic applies to all business models. He shows how to turn mundane transactions into memorable moments."

—**John R. DiJulius III,** author of *The Customer Service Revolution*

"Phil Mershon has crammed decades of event-planning experience into this must-have guide, your go-to source for all aspects of event planning."

—**Dan Gingiss,** bestselling author of *The Experience Maker: How to Create Remarkable Experiences That Your Customers Can't Wait to Share*

"This is the book I've been waiting for! Phil Mershon has finally bottled his genius insights with entertaining stories and metaphors. This book is a godsend. It is exactly what I need to plan my next *Unforgettable* experience."

—**Sigrun Gudjonsdottir,** bestselling author of
Kickstart Your Online Business, business coach, TEDx speaker

"*Unforgettable* is the event-marketing cookbook you've been looking for. It's filled with practical, hard-earned lessons from running one of the world's largest marketing conferences for a decade. Phil spends as much time dissecting things that went wrong as he does celebrating successes—and in those failures, you learn the nuances of the event business. With checklists and exercises, *Unforgettable* is necessary reading for anyone in the events industry."

—**Christopher Penn,** author of *AI for Marketers*, and
cofounder and Chief Data Scientist of Trust Insights

"*Unforgettable* shows event managers how to mix the right ingredients. Understand the science behind creating great sessions that inspire your attendees to make connections and take action long after they end. Don't let your attendees sleepwalk through your event and mistake laundry chutes for toilets! (Yes, that story is in here!)"

—**Andy Ho,** VP of Learning Experience and Innovation

"As a data scientist, I believe in creating consistent processes. As a chef, I love to make delicious meals. *Unforgettable* brings science and art together to show how to consistently design impactful events. Study it. Devour it."

—**Dennis Yu,** bestselling author of
The Definitive Guide to TikTok Advertising

"In *Unforgettable*, Phil Mershon weaves a timeless collection of insights. You'll be challenged to understand the culture of your events for long-term sustainable success that will impact attendees for life."

—**Andy Paschke,** Assistant Managing Director of Sales,
Hilton Worldwide Sales

"I'm thrilled to have my students—who will be creating and implementing future events—read and internalize *Unforgettable*. It's a must-have manual for creating and executing extraordinary, life-changing events!"

—**Dr. Jen Bennett,** professor of strategic communication

"*Unforgettable* provides a framework for focusing through the lens of attendees, resulting in memorable experiences that lead to a positive impact on the bottom line."

—**Jillian Vorce,** coauthor, *20/20 Mindsight*,
Chief Handshaker, and strategic advisor

"What I love most about this book is that it shares big ideas to implement starting today. Great experiences mixed with business thinking can lead to true success for your event."

—**Will Curran,** founder & Chief Event Einstein of Endless Events

"*Unforgettable* is the modern manual for event brand management. This definitive guide reignites your focus on critical details to distinguish your brand and culture from every other."

—**Elizabeth Allen,** author, *The Economy of One*

"No event organizer wants to spend hours planning only to have attendees walking out and forgetting it a day (or less) later. Packed with both big ideas and small details that make a surprisingly massive impact, *Unforgettable* is the bible of event planning."

—**Lizzie Williamson,** event energizer, founder of Two-Minute Moves

"From calculating sensory stimuli and proxemics to innovating the speaker green room, *Unforgettable* is everything you didn't know you needed. It includes must-have recipes, compelling observation, crisis management, and meticulous instruction. Whether you're looking to level up your next Meet Up or planning a multi-day global conference, *Unforgettable* will take you through every important step in event planning, and living up to its own name."

—**Miri Rodriguez,** senior storyteller at Microsoft

UNFORGETTABLE

The Art and Science of
CREATING MEMORABLE EXPERIENCES

PHIL MERSHON

48 DAYS PRESS
A BRANDED IMPRINT
OF MORGAN JAMES

NEW YORK

LONDON • NASHVILLE • MELBOURNE • VANCOUVER

Unforgettable

The Art and Science of Creating Memorable Experiences

© 2024 Philip J. Mershon

Published in New York, New York, by 48 Days Press, a branded imprint of Morgan James Publishing. Morgan James is a trademark of Morgan James, LLC. www.MorganJamesPublishing.com

Proudly distributed by Publisher's Group West.

Morgan James BOGO™

A **FREE** ebook edition is available for you or a friend with the purchase of this print book.

_____

CLEARLY SIGN YOUR NAME ABOVE

Instructions to claim your free ebook edition:
1. Visit MorganJamesBOGO.com
2. Sign your name CLEARLY in the space above
3. Complete the form and submit a photo of this entire page
4. You or your friend can download the ebook to your preferred device

ISBN 9781636981017 paperback
ISBN 9781636981024 ebook
Library of Congress Control Number: 2022949594

Cover & Interior Design by:
Christopher Kirk
www.GFSstudio.com

Morgan James PUBLISHING Builds with... **Habitat for Humanity** Peninsula and Greater Williamsburg

Morgan James is a proud partner of Habitat for Humanity Peninsula and Greater Williamsburg. Partners in building since 2006.

Get involved today! Visit: www.morgan-james-publishing.com/giving-back

DEDICATIONS

To Audrey: thank you for always believing I could do this, even when I didn't.

*In memory of Tracey Brouillette, who started us a sales representative
but became my friend as she created unforgettable experiences
for me almost every time we were together.*

TABLE OF CONTENTS

Acknowledgments xv

Forewords. xix

Introduction xxiii

Chapter 1: No More Boring Events 1

Section 1: Becoming Unforgettable. 11

Chapter 2: What Makes an Experience Unforgettable 13

Chapter 3: The Science of Remembering. 29

Chapter 4: Overcoming Your Enemies. 39

Section 2: Baking a Memorable Experience .55

Chapter 5: The Art and Science of Creating a Memorable Experience 57

Chapter 6: Getting Your Crew Ready to Bake 71

Chapter 7: Your Main Ingredient: Content that Produces Dough. 83

Chapter 8: Connections That Make the Difference 101

Chapter 9: Event Culture: A Little Yeast Going a Long Way. 111

Chapter 10: Creating Conditions for Change: Expecting Serendipity 135

Chapter 11: Crafting Your Customer Journey 143

Section 3: Creating Your Recipe 159
Chapter 12: How to Create Your Recipe 161
Chapter 13: Becoming Unique: What If Everyone Sang Your Song? 173
Chapter 14: Become the Only One: Finding Your Secret Ingredient 183
Chapter 15: Amplifying Your Event: Making it Shareable. 189

Section 4: Conclusion 199
Chapter 16: Mixing it All Together 201

Appendices 213
Next steps—Contact Phil 215
DRIED to TAST-E matrix 217

About the Author 219
About the Illustrator 221
Introducing Rembrandt 223
Endnotes. 225

ACKNOWLEDGMENTS

Every book is a journey. And just like every epic journey, it can't be undertaken alone. I've had cheerleaders, mentors, guides, and even friendly competitors encouraging me along the way. While there's no way I'll remember everyone, here are some who stand out.

To you, the reader, I thank you for taking the time to read this life work. Whether you get a tip or it changes your paradigm about experiences, I hope you find the value you need for this stage of your journey.

Dr. Steve Brown was the first person who said I would write multiple books over twenty years ago. I didn't believe him because I avoided writing after getting C's in grade school and beyond. Steve, I guess you were right! Thanks for believing in me and praying for me. I hope I didn't screw it up!

Pete Vargas, Michael Port, and Dennis Yu all challenged me to document my process. Thanks for the challenge and support along the way.

When I started getting "best training ever" accolades back at Koch Industries, Ching Lim, Walt Malone, and Dick Anderson challenged me to keep getting better.

Michael Stelzner gave me freedom and encouragement to create the magic and then to write this book. Mike, thanks for always believing in me.

Sigrun, you told me I have a book in me. Thanks for encouraging me to keep working on it when the writing became hard.

Angus Nelson, Adam Jones, Mike Rayburn, Elizabeth Allen, and Michael King all coached me at various stages of this process. Thanks for pushing me beyond my limiting beliefs.

Jaci Feinstein and Elise Rollinson, thanks for being my "right hand" in the early days. Nicole Sloane and Joanne Watt, thanks for pushing me to flesh this out. Lori Feinstein thanks for seeing my value and giving me space to create.

Jillian Vorce and Ambassador Mike Bruny, thanks for challenging me to think more deeply and intentionally about networking than I ever dared.

I thank John Vitale for the riveting conversations about event musicology and creating the film score for events. You have awakened in me a hunger for much greater impact than I knew possible.

To the Man in the Pew Fellowship, thanks for the consistent encouragement, belief, and creativity you offered when I wasn't sure I could or should do this.

Reggie Kidd, thanks for letting me help with your book over twenty years ago as you showed me what it takes and that it's worth it.

To all the people I interviewed along the way, including Jon Berghoff, Andrew Gough, Baker Bettie, Josh Allen, Liz Lathan, Richard Kidd, Andy Sharpe, Tom Spanos, Mimika Cooney, Delise Simmons, and so many more: Thanks for the generosity of your time and the insights you added. This book couldn't happen without your contributions.

Dan Miller and Scott McKain, you guys have blown me away with your effusive praise for this project. I sent it to you with trepidation, and you returned it with overwhelming praise. I'm humbled and honored beyond belief.

Jennifer Harshman, your editing has made this book shine. You were the first person to actually say that I'm a writer. Before that, I would have said that writing is just one of the knives on my Swiss Army Knife, but now I own that label of writer just as proudly as the first day I said, "I'm a jazz saxophonist."

Joel Comm and Karen Anderson (literary agent), I thank you for introducing me to the Morgan James Publishers family. To David, Jim, Gayle, Naomi, and the rest of the MJ team: thanks for believing in me as an author and sticking with me over a much longer cycle than we originally signed up for!

I couldn't have written this book without the constant encouragement and belief of my wife and life partner, Audrey. You stood with me when my arm went numb, when I had to get injections, through COVID, through unspeakable valleys, and to the peaks of the highest mountains. Thank you for holding down the fort and giving me space to create this. I love you.

Finally, I acknowledge my Lord and Savior, Jesus Christ, as the one who ultimately gave me the abilities to write, create, organize, and communicate. I know that I was uniquely designed to create this book (and hopefully more), and I'm eternally grateful.

FOREWORD

As someone who has worked to create a massive number of meaningful connections, I have attended an untold number of seminars, conferences and networking events. Some I barely remember. Others created memories that are fresh in my mind years after the event occurred.

Reading *Unforgettable* has helped me recognize the magic ingredients. And no, it's not just the great speakers and the great content they worked so hard to prepare. More than anything, I find it was the experience around the events that made them memorable.

In this eye-opening book, Phil walks us through a recipe for including repetition, emotion, sensory integration, and unconventionality as the ingredients for creating memorable experiences.

For years, I held events on our Tennessee property in an old barn we called The Sanctuary. We retrofitted that old barn as a matter of inexpensive convenience and only in retrospect have I recognized the magic we stumbled onto. Yes, we had great content and wonderful presenters, but the stories I hear years later are of attendees having a profound insight while walking the nature trails, or while stuffing their face with mulberries from the large tree on our property, or from their first thrill of flying down a zip line. We had bonfires where everyone sat on straw bales in the darkness while sharing a painful story. We created fun eating adventures with an Italian lady who prepared an incredible meal in exchange for getting the group input on the growth of her business. We walked back our neighbor's long lane for a meal that came right from their garden. At one event, we shared a Sabbath meal, where we observed the overflowing cup as a reminder that we serve best from a full cup.

During a two-day training for coaches, my 4-yr-old granddaughter burst through the door, announcing that we needed to have a frog funeral. Sixty people immediately stood up and followed her to the spot where she had laid the frog to rest. We had a short ceremony, sang a song together, and returned to our training. I doubt anyone there has forgotten that funeral, as it was unexpected and unconventional.

We've had attendees go on e-bike rides together and kayaking as a way of getting to know each other before the event "content" is presented. A doctor speaker had us all remove our shoes and walk in the grass as a way of encountering being "grounded."

This book you are about to read is filled with riveting examples of methods that have been used, not only in conferences, but also in restaurants, staff retreats, worship events, and virtual gatherings.

If you want your message to be heard, wrap it in an experience that your attendees will never forget.

I've been to events coordinated by the author. He speaks from a proven background of creating events that are informative but also memorable. Follow this recipe for planning your own events that are designed to not only inform but also to transform your attendees, and to allow you to thrive and prosper as the brilliant organizer.

Dan Miller, *New York Times* bestselling author
of *48 Days to the Work You Love*

FOREWORD

Some books make a contribution. Other books launch a revolution. *Unforgettable*: *The Art and Science of Creating Memorable Experiences* is that groundbreaking, radically pioneering book for the events industry. It challenges you to make a bold pledge: *"No more boring meetings!"*

Yet, if you're like me, you've encountered many books that promise you'll attain a goal, then fail to deliver the precise process for its achievement.

That's what makes *Unforgettable* iconic. Phil inspires you to unleash your inner Picasso of events while he also provides the paints, brushes, and canvas—the *details*—required to craft a meeting into an artful masterpiece.

I've been honored to appear on programs that Phil has designed. They are unforgettable—every element feels scientifically engineered for distinction. Phil walks his talk. He has delivered the very aspects he will inspire you to create. He clearly teaches you how it is done.

After 3,000 professional presentations worldwide to audiences as large as 20,000, I have a single regret: I wish every meeting professional could have read *Unforgettable*. It's the best book in the history of event planning.

Over twenty years ago, I wrote my first business book, *ALL Business is Show Business*, from my conviction that creating experiences was the most critical aspect of organizational success. Philip Mershon elevates that concept to a more significant level with *Unforgettable*. Whether planning a small gathering or an enormous convention, I promise you need this book!

Scott McKain, Founder & CEO of The Distinction Group,
bestselling author of *ICONIC: How Organizations and Leaders Attain, Sustain, and Regain the Highest Level of Distinction*
Las Vegas, Nevada

INTRODUCTION

I'll never forget Cannon Beach, Oregon. That's the first place I saw "time stand still." I was attending a retreat at a conference center. We had a break after dinner, and I decided to stroll along the beach. Over the next twenty to thirty minutes, I watched a magnificent sunset scene unfold as it continuously adapted to the shifting winds and rotation of the earth. It made me sing and dance—and I'm a terrible dancer.

In the early 2000s, I found myself frustrated by a situation at my current employer. Dr. Steve Brown challenged me to become the employee of the month, and then he said something that has stuck with me, "You never know when fifteen minutes will change your life."

As far back as 1996, I received praise from new employees at Koch Industries for running the best training event they'd ever attended. People also walked away from Social Media Marketing World saying, "Best conference ever." At first I thought this was hyperbole or that the bar must be pretty low. But after a while, I started to think about what I do that makes events special.

In 2017, I set out to write a book about how to make time stand still. After a while, I realized that's not the goal. I knew I couldn't literally accomplish that, but even figuratively, I discovered that experience is a by-product of circumstances far beyond my influence or control. So instead, I shifted to focusing on memorable and even unforgettable experiences. At the encouragement of Joel Comm and Karen Anderson, I pursued Morgan James Publishers as a publisher in 2019.

Were it not for the global pandemic of 2020, this book would have started the publication process in the summer of 2020. But it's a much more coherent book as a result of having two more years to work on it.

The Format

As you start to devour this book (yes, you will find a plethora of dad jokes inside!), you'll discover that baking bread is a central theme. Here's the simple reason: you can teach a ten-year-old child to bake a loaf of bread that is edible, but creating an exquisite artisanal loaf requires a baker who has put in their 10,000 hours of practice and study. Imagine being able to shorten that learning curve by studying with someone who has lived by the oven.

One of my friends told me that's what I've done for you. I've taken my 30,000 plus hours and lessons I've learned from many friends, books, and sessions, and compiled it into sixteen chapters. I hope that in a few hours, you'll be able to avoid many of the mistakes I've made and learn to focus on the things that cause an event to truly create lasting transformation.

Every chapter ends with a "Bread Bite." This is a chance to dig into the material immediately. In my experience, it can feel like inoculation when you read a book and don't do anything with what you learned. I've tried to help you get some immediate nutritional value.

Many of the chapters reference bonus materials that are available at philmershon.com/unforgettable/bonus. The password is: breadbites.

Let's go bake some unforgettable events!

Chapter 1:

NO MORE BORING EVENTS

I'll never forget April. She and I started chatting while waiting for the session to start. I told her I'm writing a book about event experience and she almost screamed, "Thank God! Please fix all the mandatory trainings my husband goes to. He dreads going, and he comes home so frustrated, I think he's going to hurt someone. I know he's worse off. I've been praying that someone would solve this problem."

No more. Let's stop creating dunkin' events.

What?

I'm talking about the boring, lukewarm, milquetoast events that people quickly forget. Events that leave attendees unchanged and even dreading the next time they "have to" attend another event.

In my corporate training days, we jokingly called this *inoculation training*. That's where the dipping imagery comes from. For example, we send people to harassment training and assume they will be changed. Or we send everyone through an orientation workshop or a management class expecting everyone will understand and apply what they learned. More often than not, it's a data dump and not a transformational experience. Even worse, the training primarily benefits the company and not the attendee.

I once asked a colleague what came to mind when she heard the word *retreat*. Her response shocked me: "Mandatory staff meetings masked as something fun."

Life is too precious and time too short to ask people to attend an event that won't inspire them, equip them, or improve them.

Let's agree we won't create dunking events anymore. Okay?

If you're a subject-matter expert creating a workshop designed to equip and transform people, how would you like to learn that the results are often not as life-changing as you think? What if you found that you're getting in your own way?

To be fair, most events aren't really terrible. Actually, a terrible event would at least be memorable and might motivate you to make change more often than a boring event. In a boring event, you just fall asleep or tolerate it as you're slowly numbed. In a terrible event, you would get upset and demand a refund or decide to do something better with your time.

In this book, I'm going to show you how to create events so memorable that they are unforgettable.

What if your event could be on the highlight reel of the year for your attendees? Even better, what if after five years, your attendees start referencing your event as one of the key pivot moments in their life or career?

In a sea of ordinary events, it's possible to create extraordinary, unforgettable events. I'd like to show you some of the ingredients I believe are necessary and some of the mistakes many events make that unwittingly undermine their success.

It's fairly easy to put together an event if you have an audience. It's harder to create a profitable event that people enjoy. It's really hard to create a transformational event that people rave about. But it doesn't have to be as hard as you think if you understand a few simple dynamics.

You might read the table of contents and think to yourself, "I don't see anything magical or different about this process." At one level you would be right. All events have many things in common. They have a start, middle, and ending. Most events have speakers, parties, food, networking, and exhibitors.

These are the primary ingredients for creating events. For an event to exist it must do these things reasonably well or attendees won't come and their bosses won't pay for the ticket.

The difference between ordinary and extraordinary events is in the details.

I may have just given away the most important lesson in this book, but you should keep reading because I'll show you which details you should pay attention to that can make your next event memorable and potentially unforgettable.

Let me illustrate with an example from outside the events industry.

Walt Disney World creates extraordinary memories that shape the fabric of a family's memories. Universal Studios, on the other hand, creates thrilling experiences that quickly fade. I'm sure the CEOs of each of these companies might differ with me, but let me explain.

Walt Disney World's focus is on the guest experience. They pay attention to the little details so that guests leave with happy memories and get at least a momentary break from the ordinary things in their lives. They use science to figure out how far apart to place trash cans and how to optimize line wait times. They create surprise and delight moments using RFID technology to have a favorite princess show up just in time for a young girl's birthday party. Lee Cockerell, former COO at Disney World, claims the magic at Disney World is very carefully crafted through strong attention to detail and constant learning from every cast member.

I'm not here to knock Universal Studios, as I happen to enjoy that experience, too. But that experience seems to be far more focused on rides and exhibits that create momentary thrills. Those memories quickly fade. Teenagers might love the thrill so much that they keep riding the same ride, but by the next day, all they have is a fleeting feeling that needs to be replaced.

When I reflect on my vacations at these resorts, I talk about the rides at Universal, but I talk about the memories at Disney. Those memories might have been made on a ride, but more often than not, they include some kind of human connection that was unexpected and welcomed.

When it comes to your event experiences, you should definitely create thrilling moments, but it's even more important to make them memorable—something they will keep talking about for months or years.

What's at Stake

This may be one of the most important things for your business to figure out. People attend events for the first time based on the promises of learning, networking, and fun experiences. But they come back because they were changed. They found important business connections or they learned something so important they need to return to learn again.

Some readers run events for professional organizations where members are required to attend for continuing education credits or to retain their member status. What if attendees looked forward to your event as much as they look forward to their favorite vacation destination? I believe this is possible. I'm not saying Fargo, North Dakota, can compete with Tahiti in terms of beauty or allure, but the event itself can be so compelling that people would travel almost anywhere. The destination and venue do matter, but not as much as you think once you've established the true value of the event.

What Makes an Event Boring

I recently asked my online community what makes an event boring. Here are some of their responses:

- Unprepared, unengaging, or uninspiring speakers
- Bad food
- Poor organization
- Passive participation
- Lack of awareness of time
- Too much sitting still
- No coffee, no Wi-Fi, or no power chargers
- Inauthentic or fake fun
- Forced or awkward networking
- Fluorescent lighting, fake plants, and bored greeters
- Long presentations and too much selling
- Attendees' mindset: "I have to go to this event" instead of understanding what's in it for them

- Not designing the event in light of different learning styles (kinesthetic, auditory, visual)
- Too much information, not enough insights
- Room layout—uncomfortable chairs, bad lighting, too tight to move around
- No community and little interaction
- Attendees not feeling valued or respected

Perhaps my favorite response came from Jon Berghoff, CEO of XChange Approach:

> "It's not boring that comes to mind. . . it's demoralizing, it's obsolete industrial age paradigms that are unconsciously guiding how we even think about these gatherings. It's the result of egocentric vs. ecocentric awareness of what is possible in a group. It's a complete disregard for the creative capacity to shift learning form passive to active (to transformational), to turn the audience into the stage, and to prioritize, design, and facilitate the kinds of conversations that unlock potential at the scale and speed that's possible, yet typically untouched."

We will address many of these things through the course of this book. Some of these issues, you'll learn, are more significant than others. But it may also depend on the experience you're designing.

The Cost of Being Boring

In the summer of 2016, my wife and I went to see two different movies within a week of each other. The first was *The Lost City of Z* and the second was *Rogue One: A Star Wars Story*. Our experiences couldn't have been more polar opposite. Here are a few comparisons:

- During *The Lost City of Z*, I got up to go to the bathroom five times (for comparison, I might have to do this once during a normal movie). During *Rogue One*, I never left because I didn't want to miss a single scene.

- 🛁 During *The Lost City*, they lost my attention. I was getting text messages, so I went to check them outside the theater. During *Rogue One*, I ignored all outside stimuli.
- 🛁 While the scenery in *The Lost City* was unparalleled, the plot left me thoroughly bored. The plot in *Rogue One* predictably followed the normal Star Wars type storyline, but it kept me intrigued with the constant motion, graphics, technology, and great acting.

I calculated the profitability of each movie based on publicly available data. Here's how it broke down:

	Attendance	Budget	Gross Income	Net Income
The Lost City of Z	1.9 Million	$30 Million	$19 Million	-$11 Million
Rogue One	100 Million	$200 Million	$1.056 Billion	$800 Million+

While you can still watch *The Lost City of Z* on Netflix, and some will still argue its merits, the numbers tell a frightening story. Others must have agreed with my verdict of boring. It wasn't bad enough to pull off the shelves, but it's certainly not unforgettable.

What does it cost to be unforgettable?

Have you ever found yourself scrutinizing your event budget in search of things you can cut to make room for new initiatives?

Don't cut the toothbrushes.

That sounds like great advice for a dental health conference, but what does that have to do with the rest of us?

Let me answer with a story.

In 2016, we were moving Social Media Marketing World from being a single-hotel event to being a citywide event (meaning people stay in multiple hotels and the meetings are in a central location—in this case, the San Diego Convention Center). As we thought through the transition, we tried to put ourselves in the shoes of attendees. We realized one benefit of a single-hotel event is that attendees could go up to their room between sessions to freshen up, change clothes, and brush their teeth. That would be much more difficult at a convention center that was at least ten to fifteen minutes away.

In order to eliminate this dilemma, we thought of ways to help. We recognized attendees are networking all day and want to have fresh breath after eating so having mints, mouthwash, toothbrushes, and toothpaste would be very important to some attendees.

Here's the economic problem: buying enough toothbrushes and toothpaste for everyone is not cheap. With some creative research, we discovered it might cost $3 per person, but for 5,000 people that would be $15,000. That wasn't in the budget.

Thankfully, not everyone needs a toothbrush and toothpaste, so we didn't need to buy thousands, but we did need to buy enough so we didn't run out. That still costs thousands of dollars. We decided to do it on a limited basis and got such strong feedback that we've now done it many years in a row.

When it came time to evaluate the budget, someone who doesn't know the backstory recently asked why we're spending so much on toothbrushes. They queried, "We're not a hotel. Can't people just bring their own toothbrushes and toothpaste?"

The short answer is, "Of course, and that's how most events answer this question. But we understand that if someone really wants to brush their teeth to feel comfortable for the rest of the day, it will take them at least thirty minutes and the likelihood of their not returning increases. That's bad for them and for us. They could miss out on the important lesson or relationship that will transform the value of the event. We lose out because every person contributes to the overall experience we are trying to create."

So how should we justify this expense if it seems unnecessary?

1. **Customer Service**—We believe strongly in anticipating needs and finding solutions that are within our means to solve. I encourage our team to "Go make someone's day." This is a relatively small expense to make someone's day. Malena attended our event in 2019, from Denmark. She came to the customer service desk asking for directions to a drugstore where she could buy a toothbrush and toothpaste since she

had left hers at the hotel. She was astonished to learn that she could walk down the hall to find mouthwash, a toothbrush, and toothpaste. She was blown away by our attention to detail. And her response leads to the second contributor to ROI.

2. **Word-of-Mouth Marketing** (no pun intended)—Malena went home and told fifty of her friends about this amazing experience she had at Social Media Marketing World. She then went on to talk about the toothbrush experience. That encounter represented our concern for her and the fact that we seemingly had thought about every detail. Several of these friends eventually attended the event.

3. **Influencer Marketing**—It always surprises me to learn what speakers and influencers notice. I was listening to a podcast episode with Jay Baer and Michael Stelzner about Jay's book *Talk Triggers*. In that episode, Jay mentioned that one of the things we are known for is having original music performed at every one of our conferences. He then went on to identify the toothbrush as an example of how we pay attention to every detail. That episode has been heard by more than forty thousand people. Who knows how many of those listeners purchased a ticket because of that specific episode, but the impact is massive.

The ROI of a Toothbrush

Here's an attempt to determine the ROI of one toothbrush:

Cost: $3 per person
Income: $1697 + 1394 + 1697 = $4788
    1 Happy Customer decides to return = $1697 retail
        —> Happy Customer tells 50 friends, and
    2 Friends purchase virtual tickets = $1394 retail.
    1 of those friends decides to attend in person = $1697

ROI: One customer's positive experience just paid for all the toothbrushes and toothpaste we needed to purchase that year.

Of course, not every toothbrush had this kind of return, and we can't completely attribute these decisions to the toothbrush, but it's clear that a $3 decision had a massive ripple effect.

Should we cut the toothbrushes?

Not as long as I'm the event director.

I believe the magic is in being consistent and wearing a big smile (after all, it makes people wonder what you've been up to).

And to wear a big smile, you need a toothbrush.

It's time to create your next unforgettable experience.

This book is broken into three primary sections. The central metaphor compares baking bread to creating a memorable event experience.

First, we'll define success; how do we know when something reaches the mark of being unforgettable? We'll review three goals and then reveal the five biggest threats to your success.

Second, we'll look at the primary ingredients when creating event experiences. Third, we'll help you create your secret recipe. This book will not give you a recipe but instead is going to teach you how to create your own recipe.

Bread Bite

Businesses that continue creating boring events will eventually fade into oblivion. Events that create transformational experiences will endure because of the power of their community.

Question: If people find your events boring, uninspiring, or forgettable, what will the consequences be for your business, message, or mission?

Exercise: Think about what a truly memorable and transformational experience for your attendees would make possible. Describe it in detail and discuss with your team.

Section I:

Becoming Unforgettable

Chapter 2:

WHAT MAKES AN EXPERIENCE UNFORGETTABLE

I'll never forget the first time I saw Ken Medema, a legendary gospel recording artist, in concert. He asked an audience member to tell him a story and then he created a beautiful one-of-a-kind song right there on the spot. That would have been awesome, but then he did it again. He took a good concert and made it unforgettable by making it highly personal and creating a shared experience that can never be repeated.

Most of our experiences are highly forgettable. Some of our negative experiences become unforgettable, and we wish we could cleanse our minds from them. But there are some experiences that we will cherish for the rest of our lives.

What makes those experiences stand out?

I believe there are three primary outcomes that when combined result in an unforgettable experience. And while we can't control these as much as we'd like, we can create the conditions. An unforgettable experience results when it is memorable, meaningful, and momentous.

Let's explore each of these three big ideas.

Big Idea #1: Powerful Memories

Our memories are imperfect. We tend to remember feelings more than facts. We select the parts of our memories that are helpful to hang onto. Negative memories give us nightmares. Needless to say, experience designers want to avoid creating negative memories. But sometimes they happen.

In 2018, we had several guests express concern about issues that threatened their personal safety. Until that time, our community seemed to gather harmoniously, so we were caught off guard. We responded as best as we could, but then we came up with strategies and policies to protect our guests and staff in the future.

Sometimes the experiences you design can be amazing for the majority but traumatic for a few. In 2019, our closing keynote speaker, Mark Schaefer, wanted to end his session in a highly memorable way. He envisioned confetti and fireworks. I worked with my team and created an indoor fireworks show (fireworks were on the screens due to fire code) with around one hundred confetti guns. It was an exciting moment. . .

Except for those with Post Traumatic Stress Disorder (PTSD). The loud popping of confetti guns reminded some of their wartime service. Others were reminded of the violence hitting churches, schools, and other gatherings at the time. I'm embarrassed to admit that we hadn't even considered this might be a problem.

In retrospect, I would still create this moment, and I would still want it to be a surprise, but I might use fewer confetti guns, and I would definitely have a warning at the start of the session that "There may be loud noises during this next session, and if you have hearing issues or PTSD, you might prefer to sit toward the back of the room." I would then instruct my team to not shoot off the confetti from the back so people can see where the sounds are coming from immediately and realize there isn't a threat.

So how do you make something memorable?

#1: Make it unusual or unexpected.

When Jesse Cole, owner of the Savannah Bananas, challenges his teams to come up with creative stunts during baseball games, he says, "Let's do something that's never been done on a baseball field before."

Very little in this world is totally new. It's all been done somewhere before, but creativity comes from finding ways to combine unexpected elements and environments in fresh ways. We often will remember these.

Think about some of your most powerful memories. See what stands out. Most likely it was either a very personal experience or it had an unexpected element.

While I was growing up, my pastor gave an illustration that stood out to me. He talked about a pastor who for his entire sermon got up and shaved in silence in front of the congregation. At the end of his "sermon," he said, "I'll bet you'll talk more about this sermon than any other sermon I've given in the last five years. But the Gospel message is even more radical than me shaving in front of you."

Just the telling of the story was memorable for me. But in seminary, I decided to take it to another level. You see, my pastor from growing up was my preaching professor. I decided during one of my sermons to actually shave as an illustration. I also did it in a couple of different churches. I heard afterward that it was one of the best sermons they had ever heard (er, seen).

Shaving isn't unusual. Shaving on stage in front of a church—that's unexpected. And yes, I used a real blade (and cut myself).

Question: As you think about your event experiences, what are ordinary things you can combine that might create an unexpected and powerful experience for your audience?

#2: Leverage the power of emotions.

Memorable experiences often evoke an emotional response. Knowing that 95% of decisions result from emotions, Haute (formerly known as Haute Dokimazo[1]) changed the way they design events. Since emotional experiences have the power to move people to action, they now focus on five central emotions through their event planning:

- Hopeful
- Adventure
- Active
- Acceptance
- Motivate

By focusing on the middle three emotions, events feel safer, and participants are more open to new ideas, partnerships, and solutions. This includes getting people out of their comfort zone, participating actively, and trying new experiments without permanently changing.

This came full circle for me while I gathered with friends. I had recently returned from seeing the Savannah Bananas play Banana Ball in Kansas City. It turns out a friend's daughter interned for the team the previous summer. During her final weekend, her mother and sister came to visit. During this visit, a family member became seriously ill back home, and the three women needed to get home immediately. But flights were sold out and unavailable for at least a day.

Enter the Savannah Bananas with the Fans First philosophy. Someone got on the phone, worked their magic, and got the three ladies on a flight within three hours. They went above and beyond in taking care of the family by taking care of hotels and other arrangements.

As I heard this story sitting in a bar, I began to cry. I was touched deeply. The bartender saw this and assumed I needed a drink. That brought about a humorous moment. Tears plus laughter led to a very memorable moment and removed the tension from the group where we could talk about some serious things.

Something I do as I plan any kind of event is map the emotional journey someone is taking. If I know I just created a meaningful moment where tears are possible, I don't want to keep creating deeply emotional moments like that. Instead, I try to move toward some lighthearted or even hilarious moments. Great movies and musicals do this—great events should do the same.

#3: Incorporate all the senses—but especially smell.

Smell bypasses the normal pathways to the brain and dramatically increases retention of information (15–30% better results). For example, I can walk into a restaurant that serves rhubarb pie, and as soon as I smell it, I'm immediately taken to my grandmother's farm in Iowa where she loved to bake. The thing is they sold that farm in 1990, and she's been dead since 2001. But the smell takes me back, and it feels like yesterday.

The senses can create a reminder of good times or can help reinforce a new experience. Experts advise avoiding complex smells and stick to a single aroma; otherwise, you will confuse your brain or fail to capture the trigger.

Taste is a whole different matter. You'll need to combine things to get a unique enough taste to create a memory trigger.

Sally Hogshead, author of *Fascinate*, once asked for a volunteer to join her on stage. She specifically looked for someone who had never tried Jäger-meister. She used this as a teaching moment to describe how a brand can use something really bad or out of the ordinary to become known. Jägermeister is a German digestif made with around 60 herbs and spices. And that word *digestif* says it all—just think really nasty cough medicine with 35% alcohol content. But for some reason, college-aged students use it as a rite of passage as they drink Jägermeister bombs, which is adding half a can of Red Bull. As for me, I will forever remember watching this lady drink a shot of Jägermeister on our stage. Her face was priceless. It was the same as watching a two-year-old try spinach for the first time—but, to her credit, the lady didn't spit it out!

Just like Starbucks, we've piped in coffee smells to our networking plaza to encourage people to stick around. We use tropical fragrances in our registration area to create a refreshing, relaxing experience. In our quiet zone, we incorporate soothing fragrances intended to calm people down. We also provide invigorating oils to our staff who might be lagging in energy.

It's worth noting that places, like Starbucks, that use smell intentionally don't allow employees to use perfumes or colognes so as to not interfere with the subtle smell of coffee to encourage people to purchase.

> **Warning:** Be careful to avoid using senses that might trigger allergies. Keep it light, and avoid chemically derived odors.

Big Idea #2: Highly Meaningful

When I gather with high school or college friends, we will inevitably revert to old ways of talking and relating that have little to do with who we have become in our careers. Why is that?

I think the answer, in part, sheds light on how we create shared meaning. When soldiers survive a battle, a middle schooler endures bullying, or a rookie makes it through his first season, there are bonds created because of the stress. These are formative times.

Should we create artificial stress to simulate the conditions where deeper meaning is created?

The answer is nuanced. Yes, we should create conditions where people can choose to enter into an experience where they might discover new insights about themselves or the world. But we can't force it upon them. In the military, everyone must endure boot camp. At a conference, retreat, or workshop, people usually have the option to leave or disengage. We should approach this more like great storytellers.

Lin-Manuel Miranda is a master at creating a nearly instant personal connection between his audience and the actors. In the musical *In the Heights*, he made numerous connections to common human themes without it feeling forced. I left the musical and could remember fourteen and there were likely many more. Here are just a few:

1. A boy loves a girl but is afraid to admit it.
2. When a girl loses her scholarship to Stanford, she faces the humiliation of failure and the courage needed to get back up.
3. We see the conflict when a character wins the lottery and could leave and go live his dream life but wrestles with how he could use that money to help people he loves.
4. One finds love in the face of poverty, adversity, and change.

If a great storyteller can create multiple levels of personal meaning, we can do the same at our events. But to create meaning, people need to feel safe and like you're watching out for them.

The importance of psychological safety

Psychological safety is a foundational principle for highly meaningful learning events. Psychological safety happens when we create circumstances where people relax because they feel protected and cared for. The desire to enter the fight, flight, or freeze mode is eliminated when people feel safe.

The children of cavemen felt safe when the threats of lions, tigers, and bears were eliminated. Children could sleep because there were watchmen on guard.

At events, people can relax when they know you've taken care of physical security and provided for basic needs like water, food, bathrooms, power, and coffee. If people have to stand in long lines for coffee, they have now entered into a basic needs state of mind and no longer feel safe. They start to wonder, "What else didn't they provide?"

Jon Berghoff, CEO of The XChange Approach, is a master at creating psychological safety so that people enter fully into the experiences he creates. In consultations with NASA, Facebook, and Google, he has enabled large groups of highly talented individuals to enter deeply productive and even transformational conversations. How does he do it?

In my observation, I see three principles at work:

1. Intentional design
2. Insatiable curiosity
3. Asking the right questions

When Jon leads an event (online or in person), he starts with music and conversation. There may be a live band or prerecorded music, but he's playing music that will set the tone for what's next. If people need to be pumped up, the music will be high energy. If the day is going to be more expansive and visionary, the music will be inspiring. At Jon's events, he commissioned a consultant to write songs just for the events that have the right lyrics and vibe.

In addition to the music, he starts with questions designed to help people get to know each other and set their intentions. By design, these questions start easy and safe. They don't require much thought, but they also aren't the "same old, same old." Jon spends a lot of time thinking about the questions he asks because he knows the right questions will get people to stay engaged. The wrong question will feel forced, and nobody likes forced networking.

Jon creates a rhythm between instruction and breakout. He provides some insights and then asks the audience to enter into reflection and conversation. Each round of this is preparing for a deeper conversation where the real issues of the day or event can be addressed.

Jon remains constantly curious and adjusts the event based on what he sees.

A story of psychological safety

Karen Potter loves to sing. At Hal Elrod's Best Year Ever event, she told her small group that while she loves to sing, she only does it for her kids before bed. Her small group encouraged her to sing for them, but she politely declined.

A while later, she shared her experience of empathic support to the entire conference of 300 people. When she got to the part about loving to sing, the audience quickly began encouraging her to sing for all of us. After some cheering and chanting, the emcee invited her up on stage to sing. One of her group members suggested she sing something simple like, "You Are My Sunshine." That's when she knew she should do it because that's the song she sings to her daughter every night.

And that's the moment where I was undone because that's the song we sang to our son for years, and we still call him "Sunshine."

The moment became powerful because she had the courage to get up there even though her true talent was hidden behind her nerves. She provided an emblem for many of us to step up to the mic when we are invited. That moment would never have happened if it weren't for the supportive environment that had been intentionally designed long before that moment. Because she felt safe, Karen will never forget that moment, and neither will I.

It works online, too! At a virtual event with Jon, I was placed in a group of four men. The first round of conversation was fun where each man shared something about himself by using an artifact from around our homes. I had my saxophone out because I was practicing for an upcoming gig, so I pulled it out and played for a minute and then told the story of when I moved to Chicago. I came from rural Georgia, where I was the only jazz saxophonist to Chicago, one of the top jazz cities in the world. Soon after moving I started booking gigs only to be told that I wasn't ready—I needed to spend a couple years wood-shedding (a.k.a. practicing on my own). That experience crushed me. In fact, it took almost ten years before I had the courage to start playing gigs again. But on this virtual call, I was excited to play for my new friends.

Sharing that story began a highly meaningful day for me. In fact, the ines-capable theme of the day was that music needs to be part of my brand and the way I show up to the world. It all started because I felt safe to share my gift with that small group.

By the end of the event, our group was assigned a project to present one of the core takeaways we had from the week. We were given seven minutes to create an experience that showcased what we learned. All the other groups led shared presentations with multiple people talking, but our group got creative. And they asked me to play the saxophone.

This experience will stick with me for life. Every time I start to doubt whether I should play saxophone or show up creatively, I remember that experience. It's one of the few places where I felt truly seen by people who didn't have any reason to doubt or diminish me.

Meaningful events create a safe place where people can discover new insights, deeper connections to their purpose, or new opportunities never considered.

Consider the emotional journey. Most people enter new contexts with a mixture of expectancy and reservations. You can influence this mix with your pre-event communication and connections.

Pre-event: During COVID-19, we all learned that we needed to address people's varied concerns over safety protocols. People decided whether to attend based on how we addressed these issues. Prior to that and since then, people have always done this, but it was more of a subconscious evaluation. If an event felt haphazard in its approach to safety, people would be more reserved.

In my days as a worship pastor, I designed programs with an ear toward the mental and emotional readiness of members to participate in what we planned next. For instance, if we started with a strong upbeat song, the next thing we did should probably not be an extended period of silence. People need time to adjust, but even more important, that's not what people are ready for. Better to follow that up with a bit slower song or a dramatic reading that matches the emotional level.

As I witnessed with the Savannah Bananas, you can manage the emotional journey of your audience and it doesn't have to take a long time to get from point A to point B.

Think about the snowball effect. Andy Stanley is credited with saying, "Do for one what you wish you could do for many." The snowball effect is the concept of starting very small and creating powerful experiences for a few people, and they will begin to pay it forward. You'll get a logarithmic effect that influences the experience for everyone.

How might we create micro experiences? At a Savannah Bananas game, the team members come into the stand to bring flowers to little girls. Another family gets to celebrate their small child as the team forms a "Circle of Life" (inspired by the opening scene of the Disney movie, *Lion King*) and lifts the child up for the entire stadium to see.

FACT: Parents in Savannah, Georgia, call to get their child on the Circle of Life list as soon as they conceive, even before getting on the preschool list.

At our events, I encourage team members to make at least one person's day every day. I give them coffee cards, but no more budget than that. Instead, I invite them to get creative. Often, it's in a service opportunity that these moments are created.

I find networking super-connectors are often the ones who can deliver this magic. Within a minute or two of talking to someone, they might hear them say they would love to meet a certain speaker or influencer. Imagine the delight when the connector takes this apprehensive guest to meet the speaker they've always admired from afar!

In the early '90s, I was an aspiring songwriter. I started a songwriting fellowship which gave me the opportunity to take voice lessons with Scott Martin, a highly respected teacher in the Christian Music Industry. I went to an industry event to see how my songs might compare to others. Scott saw me lingering outside a concert and asked me if I'd like to meet Phil Keaggy, one of my heroes. Before I could think about it, I said sure. He quickly ushered me into the "green room," where Phil was jamming with some musicians. When Scott introduced me, Phil assumed I was a guitar player and handed me his guitar so I could play with them. I demurred because I knew I'm like a kindergartener on guitar compared to him. But the impression will last forever because Scott gave me a one-of-a-kind experience with a hero, and I quickly learned that this hero is just like me.

Use your data. When you market your event, your marketing team will often formulate a set of marketing avatars. Use the demographic data and some personal research to create a more detailed story about the people coming and how you might make their day.

For example, for one of our events, we know our primary avatar is a female marketer between the ages of 35–50 who works for someone else's business. From that information, we surmise that she is probably a mother and likely left a couple of children behind with her husband. When we talk to our sponsors about the types of swag to bring, we encourage them to have gifts that moms can take their children. We also create a moment during one of the keynotes where the wife can send a text message to her husband thanking him for letting her spend these days investing in herself.

What do you know about your audience that can help you create experiences that will be meaningful for your audience?

Find moments of communal relevance. In 2020, we wrote a musical parody based on *Annie* that included a moment where we thanked Mark Zuckerburg for making the algorithm so complicated so we could keep our jobs. The audience roared. It was an industry inside joke that might have been misunderstood somewhere else.

But I would encourage you to avoid making inside jokes on stage that are only understood by a few people. Use humor to bring people together. Getting political or religious can go south very quickly, as one of our speakers learned when he literally alienated half of an 800-person room and saw at least 200 people get up and walk out within mere minutes of making some strong, politically charged comments.

If you know you have some large groups attending your event together, find ways to create a shared experience for them. For instance, we will sometimes get 20–30 members of the US State Department attending. We find out what might make their experience especially meaningful and try to make it happen. Often, it's merely an introduction to a speaker or two who are usually delighted to have the opportunity to serve an audience like this.

Leverage your location. If you host your event in Southern California but keep everyone inside a concrete expo hall for three days, you've done them a disservice. Find ways to get people outside, and leave them time to explore and enjoy. If you have the budget (or a sponsor), host an event in a cool location that will become a talking point. For instance, Content Marketing World often hosts a party at the Rock and Roll Hall of Fame.

Create stories. An emcee for an event where I spoke went out of his way to create a unique story for every speaker he introduced. He changed his attire and coordinated his walk-on music. For one speaker, he dressed as a baseball player because he knew the speaker would "knock it out of the park." When he introduced me, he dressed ready to dance and got the audience on their feet enjoying themselves so that their blood was pumping. And the GIFs from many of these moments were priceless and became easy ways for people to talk about things that happened.

Big Idea #3: Shareworthy Moments

In the summer of 2017, I had one of the most memorable convergence moments of my career. I was sitting at a Corporate Event Marketers Association (CEMA) event when I heard a phrase pop in my head: "Make time stand still."

I was watching a master emcee create aha moments for the audience. Something clicked. I immediately remembered two incidents where this idea gelled:

First was the story I told about the sunset on the Oregon coast. Thinking back on that time, I was in a moment of transition in my career and feeling a bit uncertain. That sunset gave me encouragement that there is something *so* much bigger going on and to not get lost in the details of my life. "Lift your eyes and enjoy the beauty around you" seemed to be the encouragement.

That's the first time where I felt like time stood still. The next was in 2006, nearly 15 years later. Music Theatre of Wichita performed the lesser-known musical, *Sweet Charity*.

The musical is mostly a lighthearted comedy about a woman named Charity who works as a dancer in a seedy dance hall. All she really wants is to find someone who will love her. Along comes Oscar, a neurotic actuary who wants to love Charity but is full of self-doubt. By the end of the musical, you realize he's more the person of ill-repute, and she's the person of character. But when

Charity asks Oscar if he could ever love someone who has lived the life she lived, he assures her that of course he will.

Near the end of the show, we get a glimpse into his heart when he asked aloud if he could ever give her the love she deserves. He asked the questions every man asks at some point in time: "Am I enough? Do I have what it takes?"

Those questions hit me hard, and I didn't want that moment to end. I knew I couldn't escape those questions. Unfortunately, the show moved on, but I'll never forget that moment. It made me wonder if I could create similar moments of transcendence at conferences.

I interviewed the artistic director, Wayne Bryant, to find out how he created that moment. Did he do anything special with the music, lighting, staging, or acting to intensify that moment? Did he try to anticipate those peak moments that might have the greatest impact?

His answer surprised me: "No. My goal is to tell the story in the best way possible. I let the story speak for itself. You had that moment stand out, but for someone else, it was a different moment. If you were to see it five times, you might notice something different each time—and possibly in an equally powerful way."

That illustrates an important point: **Not all moments are remembered equally.**

In their book, *The Power of Moments*, Chip and Stan Heath describe research they did for Disney to understand how people remember their park experiences. While it's called The Magic Kingdom, not all moments are magical. In fact, some are forgettable. Others are even negative. I mean, who likes to stand in line for an hour in the heat? When you add crying children and expensive food, it can feel like a bust.

But when asked about their experience, park guests remember things like meeting Cinderella, seeing the fireworks, and going on the Space Mountain ride. Those were all peak experiences. Those experiences end up defining the experience. That's why the Disney theme parks spends lavishly on the light parade and fireworks show and creating new unforgettable ride experiences.

Events are a series of moments. A conference, workshop, or retreat isn't a moment—it's a series of moments. There are inevitably going to be lulls in the action. Some of this is needed. Just as an athlete can't push hard for endless hours without periods of rest, conference attendees need variety in their pacing. It can be helpful to think of your event like a roller coaster with a long ride to the top and then many peaks, valleys, spins, and surprises. **Thoughtful event planners emphasize the key moments and create contingency plans for negative moments.**

Brick and Mortar

When scheduling an event, consider how the elements of the event fit together. Often times, event organizers put a lot of effort into the building blocks (I call them bricks) of the event, such as sessions, parties, and other workshops. And that's good. That's what people paid for, and we all want those to go very well.

But many event organizers underthink the gaps between the bricks—the mortar, or micro experiences. This results in a disjointed experience and lots of awkward pauses. Or feeling like you're less than human.

I was speaking with a friend recently who attended a first-time event. The event sold far more tickets than expected and didn't have enough seats for the people in attendance. As a result, the hallways were jam-packed between sessions. There was nowhere to sit down and no room to stop and have a conversation. People felt like cattle being prodded.

Do you enjoy being herded? Did you sign up to be a human herder?

Bread Bite

When you create powerful memories that are highly meaningful, you formulate impactful moments. If you create enough of these, the event will become unforgettable, and the things you hope people will forget will also become less important.

Question: What makes events meaningful to you?

Exercise: Think back on a conference experience that has been important to you. Make a list of the first ten things you remember about the event. Don't take more than three minutes to do this.

Once you have a list, circle the top three items that you think had the biggest impact on why the event was memorable and impactful. Describe in detail what you remember about each of those three items. Who was there? What were they wearing? What were you doing? How did you feel? What can you smell? What do you see and hear? Are there any lingering tastes in your mouth?

Why do you think it was so meaningful for you? What was going on for you? Did the event do something to make it a personalized experience for you? Can you remember anything that went wrong? Why do you think you're more focused on the impactful moments?

Once you answer those questions for each of the three peak experiences, look for trends. These should be your starting place for your next event design.

Chapter 3:

THE SCIENCE OF REMEMBERING

I'll never forget attending a Chicago Bulls game with my son. He loves basketball, so I was excited to watch a good game. But it didn't take long for the game to take a backseat to the games within the game. The organizers masterfully kept all the demographics engaged by having crowd engagement activities on every break imaginable. They had dog tricks, human tricks, I spy cams, trivia contests, cheering matches, and much more. I've been to hundreds of college games and a few NBA games, but I had never seen such an intentional display of engagement tactics—until I went to a Savannah Bananas game.

I once asked Scott Page, saxophonist for Pink Floyd, Supertramp, and Toto, to describe his most memorable concert experience. He immediately referenced the Pink Floyd concert in Venice, Italy in 1989.

Desiring to perform in peculiar places for avid fans, the organizers arranged for a floating stage to be pulled near St. Mark's Basin. The timing was during the Feast of the Redeemer, so the local community was divided. Some were concerned the band would cause damage to their historic mosaics, statues, and buildings. Others advocated the need to keep up with modern times.

As a concession, the band agreed to lower its decibels from 100 to 60 and arranged for 3 barges to be pulled together to create a massive floating stage over 300 feet long by 79 feet wide and 79 feet tall.

The concert itself was memorable because of the historic setting, but what was unforgettable was the way 200,000 people showed up three days early and created a weeklong event. Between the political battles and the sheer volume of food, bathrooms, trash, and boats, the event became epic. All the local officials resigned after the event in response to the public outrage. The band and fans remember the concert as the highlight of a lifetime.

This event began for Scott a lifetime of mashing up the familiar to create new experiences that expand the mind and push into new frontiers. That's what he does today through his company Think:Exp.

Making Something Memorable

**"Shared experiences create memories. Memories cement learning moments.
Learning moments create change."**
—Liz Lathan, cofounder, Haute

Scientists have discovered three distinct types of memory: the ability to recall facts (declarative memory), personal experiences, and skills such as riding a bicycle. Memory is also stored in short and long-term forms. **The depressing truth for event planners is that most people forget 90% of what they learn within 30 days of the event.**

The secret to creating a lasting memory involves a combination of four forces: repetition, emotion, sensory integration, and unconventionality. Let's explore each.

Repetition

It seems obvious that repetition is crucial for remembering facts and mastering a skill like playing a musical instrument, but the role in keeping experiential memories alive may be less obvious. But try this experiment. . .

Think about your earliest childhood memory. How old were you? What were you doing? Where were you living? Can you remember what you were wearing? Who was with you?

Let me tell you mine and then I'll share an important lesson about memory.

My first memory is of me driving my dad's classic '55 Chevy down the driveway. I was three years old. It was scary and exciting as I drove down the driveway until my parents rescued me. I was wearing my brown overalls, and my younger brother and sister were in the backseat screaming (with delight, I like to think).

What really happened?

The three of us kids were waiting in the car to go to church or the store (no one remembers). I jumped into the driver's seat and pretended I was driving the car. I never engaged the engine and we never moved. But rehearsing that daydream for years made it seem like it really happened.

The lesson: Many of our experiential memories are shaped by how we retell the story. The emotions rarely change, but the details become blurred and shifted by how the story is told. I have many memories from my childhood that are almost entirely based on having heard the story told so many times that it seems I remember it when I know it's actually not possible that I was aware of what was happening.

Event organizers should encourage attendees to start telling their stories right away about what was important and worth remembering.

How can we reinforce repetition inside events?

Consider finding ways to engage all three learning styles (the fourth style of read/write is less relevant for most events). **Visual learners** want to see something, so invite them to draw a picture. **Verbal learners** like to hear and talk; get them to create a story that they tell to other attendees several times. **Kinesthetic learners** like to do something tangible, so get them to build something or try something with their hands. Maybe give them Play-Doh to build a model of what they learned.

Secondly, repetition is something we have to **commit** to doing. Invite attendees to do something daily for 30 days. Ask them to make an appointment to follow up with a speaker, sponsor, or attendee in the next seven days.

Challenge them to create an article or video to document what they learned. Maybe have a contest.

As a marketer and event professional, Megan Powers suggests creating channels like a hashtag where participants can share their stories. It's also powerful to have teams on-site to document testimonies and stories. Professional videographers and journalists can be powerful allies to this end.

Following the epic Haute Secret Family Reunion, Nicole Osibodu (one of the co-founders) challenged attendees to create a video testimony and the top three videos received a prize. Additionally, Liz Lathan invited participants to send in a testimonial quote and she shared these with graphics on LinkedIn. It became very shareable content.

Many of us were deeply impacted by that experience. In fact, 54 of us continue to actively stay in touch through a Whatsapp group. Here's how I summarized my unforgettable experience:

> "I went into this experience expecting it to be memorable. How awesome to go somewhere unknown with a new group of event professionals?! But what I didn't expect was for the experience to last over 4 weeks from the wild crazy ride of getting my passport renewed to having a train canceled due to bad weather to amazing friendships with some of the smartest event family I could know and then to getting snowed into Chicago after the event ended. I'd do it all again. I learned the importance of showing up powerfully. I learned how to remain flexible and trust the process. I learned to keep my eyes open as there is beauty all around you. I'm changed by the HD family. And I wouldn't have it any other way."

Jeff Hurt of Velvet Chainsaw provides another way to create meaningful repetition. At the conclusion of events he challenges attendees to schedule a follow-up call or email with a fellow attendee 21 days after an event to check in for a progress report on specific commitments made.

Emotion

We tend to remember things that create a strong emotional reaction. That could be joy, anger, delight, fear, frustration, anxiety, or elation. One of the reasons it's challenging for event organizers to overcome negative experiences at their event is because negative emotions tend to feed more negative emotions. But it's not impossible!

As explained by Chip and Dan Heath in their book *The Power of Moments*, you can cause negative memories to slip into the background by creating enough powerful and surprising experiences for your customers. Last memories can be one of the best ways to do this as Disney does through their closing parade and fireworks show.

If you're wondering about the importance of emotion in business, look no further than the research done by the team at Haute. Liz Lathan and team created a measure called Return on Emotion that calculates all the ways emotional connection and impact lead to more impactful and profitable relationships with your best customers.

At one of our recent conferences, I found a frustrated customer wandering around our exhibit floor. I stopped to talk with her and discovered she hadn't attended any sessions that were valuable. She was upset enough that she was ready to leave. By asking some questions, I learned that what she really wanted was advanced training on a specific topic. I opened our program with her and suggested three speakers I knew could help her if she was willing to stay after their talks to ask questions. She didn't know any of those speakers, but upon going to their sessions, her conference experience was transformed.

It took time to listen carefully, acknowledge the problem, defuse the emotion, and then creatively find a solution that would surpass her expectations. It's not always easy to do this, but when we do, we can reverse the negative emotions and create a lasting positive memory.

"Listen carefully, respond creatively."
—Darren Ross, CEO, Magic Castle

Sensory integration

Many scientists have documented the positive benefits of integrating multiple senses to boost learning and memory. For example, Dr. Richard Mayer has famously shown that the integration of visual and audio information increases retention by anywhere from 50 to 75%.

What event organizers often forget is the power of smell. The nose creates a direct path to the amygdala. In his book *Remembering Things Past*, Marcel Proust first spoke about how smell can elicit long-lost memories.

The use of smell at events can be powerful, but it can also be dangerous since we live in an age of many allergic sensitivities. We creatively worked with one venue to cook large vats of coffee and strategically placed fans to blow the aroma through a room to enhance the coffee break to hopefully keep people lingering in conversation. We've also used essential oil diffusers to create a refreshing tropical vibe as people arrive to help them relax. At other events, I've strategically placed bread makers to signal the brain that lunch is coming soon (beware as this can also become a distraction!).

To illustrate the power of smell, let me share an experience I had today. I drove down the road and became aware of the smell of rotten eggs (sulfur). My mind instantly remembered waking up in Kenya to the smell of the local sugar refinery where sulfur is used in the refining process. My stomach became upset as I recalled awaking many days with stomach cramps caused by a poor diet composed of rice, beans, and bananas. I remembered many other things about the experience—all triggered by the smell of sulfur.

Many stores use the power of smell to influence how people purchase, so be careful that you're not manipulating and instead use smell to reinforce important memories. If there is a natural aroma you can use during certain key moments in your event, it can have a profound impact on the likelihood that people will remember other experiences.

Unconventionality

"There's nothing new under the sun" is a famous ancient proverb. It's still true today; however, I do think you can create new experiences by combining familiar elements into something new. Scott Page is doing this with Think:Exp by bringing the familiar music of Pink Floyd into a virtual reality immersive experience that will challenge the way you think and see the world.

You can do something similar with your event.

Start with something that seems familiar and comfortable. Then ask yourself what you could combine that with.

Let me provide an example from the world of music and entertainment.

Mike Rayburn is a performance artist and comedian. He famously combines two or more familiar songs or artists and creates a brand-new experience as a result. One of my favorite examples is his performance of *Green Eggs and Ham* from Dr. Seuss as if performed by Led Zeppelin. Look it up on YouTube.[2]

I will never forget the time I saw Mike perform the song "The Devil Went Down to Georgia" all by himself on guitar. He played the dueling violin battle (on guitar). He played all the parts of the band members. He sang everything. It took him a year to learn to do this because he asked the all-important question, "What if?"

So, to create an unconventional and memorable experience, start with something familiar and comfortable and then ask yourself what you could combine that with. Derek Thompson, author of *Hit Makers: How Things Become Popular*, suggests creating moments of surprising familiarity. Use what he calls sneaky familiarity to make people feel comfortable in a world of new ideas and experiences.

"The aesthetic aha is that moment of thrilling recognition that you are found in a lost world, it is the moment when novelty yields itself into familiarity, and it is that moment that makes a story irresistible."—Derek Thompson

Liz Lathan does this at Haute training events. She decided to challenge the way we always do event registration. She asked herself what if she combined event registration with a high-end restaurant experience where you check in with a *maître d'* and then are seated at a table with preassigned seats while hosts go to get your event materials. In the meantime, you engage in conversation over food and drink with other event guests.

Personalization is the X Factor. Event technologist Shing Wong suggests that personalization trumps everything else in terms of making an event memorable.

"For example, everyone can attend a basketball game and if the team wins, everyone may remember that game. But if maybe the game was the first time you treated your dad to a game, it's infinitely more memorable to you. Although the experience of being there to see a winning game was shared with thousands, it was all the more special and memorable because that very game was one that you had a much higher purpose and personal investment in. Personally, this is exactly what happened for me last year when I took my dad to a Warriors-Spurs playoff game."

What can event organizers do to make their events deeply personal? Perhaps you schedule at a time when people can make the trip a family vacation. Or maybe introduce a way for attendees to visually state their goals and then give a way to celebrate their successes.

Importance of Remembering

In the classic children's book, *The Silver Chair* by C. S. Lewis, Aslan gives Jill the task of remembering four signs that will guide their journey to rescuing Prince Rillian. She diligently rehearsed these for days, but she failed to teach them to Eustace and Glimfeather. Slowly, she forgot to rehearse them and when it came time for her to use the signs, she had either forgotten them or discombobulated them so that they got into deep trouble.

When people leave our events, they often have learned transformational lessons and made important friendships, but far too often these discoveries are lost because attendees fail to move from experience to memory. Through a careful design of the experience that continues long after the event concludes, we can make these memories lasting and life-changing.

One week later

Most events, including ours, falter when it comes to the post-event experience. We have a great pre-event buildup. Our on-site experience might be amazing. But as soon as people leave, it's easy for all of us to move on to what's next.

Jesse Cole, owner of the Savannah Bananas, decided to change this. He commissioned his team to create a new video every weekend that included highlights of that weekend's games. Those were included with the team's newly minted song, "One Week Later" a remix of the BareNakedLady song by the same title. Fans love it because the images are things they will remember. They might even see themselves.

Bread Bite

Question: What can you do to help your attendees remember your experience?

Exercise: Start with the end in mind. Choose one thing you want people to remember about your event. It could be a skill, memory, or piece of knowledge.

Start by picturing what people are doing 30 days after your event with that memory, skill, or knowledge. Now let's trace that memory back to its origin:

- 21 days post-event—who did they talk with today to keep this alive?
- 14 days post-event—what are they doing today to keep that memory alive?
- 7 days post-event—what were they doing for the last seven days to internalize this memory?
- 1 day after the event—how are they telling this story? Where are they practicing this skill? What are they doing with this knowledge?
- The day they learned this—who were they with? How did you create space in the event to begin the internalization process?

At each one of these intervals, how might you create prompts or opportunities to strengthen these memories?

Chapter 4:

OVERCOMING YOUR ENEMIES

I'll never forget riding the Finnish Fling at Worlds of Fun in Kansas City. The cylindrical ride is based off the German ride, the Rotor. With everyone standing around the edge, the ride slowly speeds up to 33 revolutions per minute where riders are suspended in a spacelike environment, and experience approximately 3 Gs of gravitational force. It's an awesome feeling (unless you have a weak heart).

What's your favorite ride at the amusement park? I think one of the first rides all of us enjoy is the merry-go-round. Carnival makers know how to keep it going at a speed that is fun for kids of all ages.

As we get older, the playground merry-go-round becomes a source of amusement as we see how fast we can make it go before we become dizzy and fall off. Without realizing it, we are experimenting with centripetal and centrifugal forces. When kept in perfect balance, these forces keep us suspended. If they get out of whack, we fall down, fall off, or get thrust to the center of the ride unable to escape.

A great event knows how to use centripetal and centrifugal forces to create that sense of suspending time. To do it, you have to know what forces you're working against and what the counterbalance is.

Let's leave the amusement park and return to our event kitchens and put on our bakers' hats.

5 Threats to Your Event

There is nothing worse than a dried-out or moldy piece of bread. Mold is easy to see, and we all know it develops when bread is left in a moist environment. A dried-out loaf of bread can happen even during the baking process. Unless you're making croutons, crumbs for your Thanksgiving turkey, or bird food, I would venture to say you like your bread to be adequately soft and moist.

Under this assumption, I'm going to summarize the threats to your event experience with the acronym DRIED. Our goal is to turn a dried-out event into a TAST-E event.

Know thine enemies. One of the worst scores to earn on an event survey is "meh." People who give you a 3 on a scale of 1 to 5 don't often leave you specific feedback. It's because they don't have much to say. It wasn't great, but it also wasn't terrible. It was like drinking lukewarm coffee.

Even bad coffee will taste okay if it's really hot—why do you think convenience stores serve it as hot as possible? It's also okay when it's served super cold with a nitrogen infusion. But when it comes to room temperature, you find out it really wasn't that good. I'll often spit out lukewarm coffee and search for a fresh cup.

When it comes to event experiences, your enemies can be described as having:

- Dullness
- Resistance
- Isolation
- Exhaustion
- Distraction

In Appendix B, you will find a matrix that helps you walk through each of these five threats and how to transform the accompanying negative beliefs into the positive outcome summarized by the word TAST-E.

- 🎂 Transformative
- 🎂 Accepting
- 🎂 Stimulating
- 🎂 Together
- 🎂 Engaging

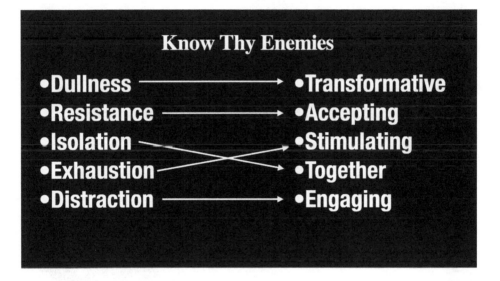

Dullness

If you're a parent, you know one of the worst things your teenager can say to you is, "I'm bored," or "That's *sooo* boring!" As we described in Chapter 1, event attendees across the board are being bored to death every day, and we seem to be okay with that.

Jesse Cole saw this happening in Savannah Bananas baseball games and decided to do something about it. Instead of three hours of confusing boredom, he shortened the game to two hours and made it fun—something that grandparents, parents, and children could all enjoy together.

Here's what the transformation might look like. Your attendees have negative and toxic beliefs and feelings that cause them to see your event as boring. Here are things they might be saying to themselves:

- Belief: I don't need this.
- Feeling: I feel misunderstood.
- Thinking: I've heard this before.
- Relating: These aren't my people.
- Action: I'd rather take a nap.

As we saw in Chapter 2, the cost of boredom is extreme. What's the solution? Make it transformative.

Transformative

To help our attendees move from seeing our event as dull to transformative, we seek to create personal meaning and significance. It starts by replacing their negative thoughts and feelings with new beliefs. Here are statements we want to see them embrace:

- Belief: This is for me.
- Feeling: I feel seen.
- Thinking: I am intrigued.
- Relation: I belong.
- Action: I want to improve.

Creating the path from A to Z is not easy or straight. If it were, everyone would be doing it. Walking that path is also highly subjective. Some of your attendees know how to extract value from any and all circumstances. They will appreciate your attempts to make it easier. There's also the truth that some people will never be pleased. Your goal is to go after the middle 80%. The top 10% will excel in almost any circumstance, and the bottom 10% will struggle anywhere they go.

This book is full of strategies that will help. In short, make it personal, relevant, provoking, relational, and exciting. Create a sense of wonder and intrigue. Do something unexpected and memorable.

In three words: **make someone's day**.

Resistance

Whether you know it or not, your event attendees are showing up with some hesitancy and resistance toward you and your event. They trusted you enough to buy a ticket and show up, but they are still waiting for you to prove that you can be trusted.

Perhaps they've heard from others some bad things about you. Maybe they had a bad experience at another event recently.

My wife and I were planning to go out to dinner recently. She suggested a restaurant we've been to many times. I initially said "yes" but upon reflection realized it didn't appeal to me at all. I couldn't figure out why until I remembered I had a bad choking attack there that caused my diaphragm to freeze up in 2018. That association—while not the restaurant's fault, other than that no one came to help me—made me want to avoid an otherwise good restaurant.

Here are some of the negative thoughts and feelings your attendees might hold toward your event:

- Belief: This is below me.
- Feeling: I feel guarded or agitated.
- Thinking: These people don't know what they're talking about.
- Relating: Nobody wants to be with me.
- Action: I feel so upset I'm going to leave.

You have no idea what resistance you have to overcome. That's why it's important that you have a strong group of friendly staff on your welcome team. This is a moment for setting the tone. It doesn't have to be a high-energy back-slapping vibe, but it should be warm, inviting, and reassuring. I'll use the word *Accepting* to convey the vibe.

Acceptance

We accept people right where they are while we try to assure them this is a safe place and we get who they are.

I like to communicate this simple message in how we act:

1. I see you.
2. I welcome you.
3. You belong.

If we've created the feeling of acceptance and openness, those negative beliefs will turn into positive statements like the following:

- Belief: I'm right where I need to be.
- Feeling: I feel accepted and affirmed.
- Thinking: I am challenged to think differently.
- Relating: There are many people here worth meeting.
- Action: I will slow down to extract as much value as I can.

Again, this can sound oversimplified. Nobody makes these internal changes on a dime. It takes repetition and consistency to help someone trust you. It starts with the very first customer service encounter they have. But the good news is that within five to seven encounters with your staff, attitudes can change. And if you find a chance to provide above-and-beyond service, you can move someone from resistance to acceptance quickly.

Don't forget your secret weapon. Your best experience evangelists are satisfied customers who keep coming back. They often have an intuitive sense of what makes the culture great and will have your back.

Isolation

There are many reasons people withdraw and isolate while at events. Let's explore a few:

- Some people don't feel like they have much to offer so they don't want to look or feel foolish.
- Others feel more advanced in knowledge and experience and don't want to waste their time talking to people who don't understand their situation.
- Probably 50% of your audience is introverted, which means they get their energy from being alone. Many people use this as permission to not engage if they also feel socially anxious.
- Starting a conversation with strangers is listed as one of the top 10 biggest fears for many people.
- Often people find it more comfortable to sit alone than with strangers.

It would be easy to look at this list and dismiss these as illegitimate or ill-founded. After all, your event will be a safe, judgment-free environment where everybody shows up and respects the opinions and experiences of others. Why would anyone possibly be afraid of strangers at our events?

It all started at home. Our parents told us to stay away from strangers. The news confirms this every day. Plus, we've all had negative experiences that reinforce the belief that stranger equals danger.

So how do we overcome this at our events where people say they are coming to network?

Do you know what my biggest fear is at a networking event? It's Card-Pushing Carl. You've met him. Within ten seconds of meeting you, he has forced a business card into your hand and is halfway through his elevator pitch.

Card-Pushing Carl doesn't help your cause. Don't let Carl be on your welcome crew. In fact, see if you can help Carl find another way to serve your event (or someone else's event).

My goal is to help attendees replace these negative views with positive beliefs, thoughts, and feelings:

- Belief: "I believe one conversation could change my life."
- Feeling: "I am seeking serendipity."
- Thinking: "Most of these people feel like I do, so I can take the initiative."
- Relating: "Every person here has a story worth hearing."
- Action: "I want them to hear my story, so I will take time to listen to other stories."

Our goal is to move people from isolation to a decision to pursue community; in short to be **together**.

Togetherness

Researchers have found that we learn much faster in community as long as we feel safe. How do we facilitate this transformation?

It starts with creating psychological safety. People need to know you're looking out for them. They want to know that the people at your event are safe and can be trusted.

Some specific ways to do this are through the use of volunteers who are friendly and the presence of security staff. The security staff don't ever have to say anything, but their mere presence lets attendees know you're looking out for them.

Use people's names when you greet them. People love to hear their names. And if you have people on your team who are really good at researching and remembering names, employ them to be on your greeting team. Politicians do this all the time. Why don't we do it at our events? Social media makes this really easy since many people have a digital presence that can allow you to get to know them. At minimum, do this with your top customers.

Another way to help your newcomers, who are most at risk of feeling isolated, is to create some form of orientation. This is a great time for people to form some new relationships and learn some basics about your event. Information is also a weapon in helping people move from isolation toward feeling together.

Some events will send out some kind of baggage tag, shirt, or hat so other attendees will recognize them at the airport as they arrive. If you've already made a few friends before you arrive, you're far more likely to feel open and safe.

One of the other strategies we employ is through our pre-event community groups. We've used Facebook groups effectively to help hundreds or thousands of attendees to feel connected. A mobile app can also do this.

If someone feels like they have two or three friends, they will feel comfortably safe and more easily choose to engage.

Exhaustion

You have very little control over how much energy people will have when they show up to your event, but you can help them manage their energy during it. If attendees are constantly yawning and looking for the coffee bar, it's likely they aren't functioning at their highest brain capacity.

> **Research:** Fatigue affects brain functioning the same as alcohol or drugs. Police officers pull over drivers who fell asleep at the wheel almost as frequently as drunk drivers. I know I've had several near accidents while trying to drive long distances on too little sleep.
>
> The Center for Disease Control (CDC) says, "Studies have shown that going too long without sleep can impair your ability to drive the same way as drinking too much alcohol. Being awake for at least 18 hours is the same as someone having a blood content (BAC) of 0.05%. Being awake for at least 24 hours is equal to having a blood alcohol content of 0.10%. This is higher than the legal limit (0.08% BAC) in all states."[3]

Let's avoid having sleepwalking accidents at our events.

When I was a kid, I had a problem with sleepwalking. I once mistook the laundry chute for a toilet—that took a while to clean up!

As an event organizer, you know it's beneficial to have your attendees alert, energized, and ready to learn. But inevitably, people show up fatigued because of all the work they had to do just so they could be away for three days. They may be drained physically and emotionally due to family issues or even personal health problems. Many of these things are beyond your control, but you can do things to improve their energy.

First, let's combat some negative thought patterns that might perpetuate a depleted energy state. Your attendees might be thinking things like these:

- Belief: I need to do everything.
- Feeling: I have FOMO (Fear of Missing Out).
- Thinking: I can sleep later, so bring on the coffee.
- Relating: Meeting new people wears me out.
- Action: Events always make me sit too long.

It's easy to read these statements and wonder how people could hold onto these beliefs. But realize you are part of the problem. If people want to stay up late and rise early, it's because you've created such a great event and community that they don't want to miss out on anything.

Perhaps the easiest way to help people is to change the narrative. If they were given $1,000 for a shopping spree at your local mall, they might find themselves tempted to overspend, but they would never feel compelled to buy everything they see. If they do, that's a mental illness, and they may need help! Most people understand the concept of budgets. You can help them spend their energy well.

We can deepen this story by taking it into the world of video games. Many games have a way to restore depleted energy reserves. It might be through winning a contest, defeating a certain enemy, or finding a prize. What if your event had energy-boosting activities built into it?

Here are some potential energy-boosting activations:

- Movement breaks—Lizzy Williamson coined the 2 Minute Movement breaks, which she does for physical and virtual conferences across the globe. Whether it's a quick movement snack or a longer yoga class or a brisk walk, movement always gets the blood flowing back to the brain.
- Quiet zone—Have a quiet area where people can grab a 20-minute power nap. This seems counterintuitive for those who see this as laziness, but the science is strong on the power of a nap—especially if you take a coffee nap by drinking 200mg of caffeine immediately before the nap.[4]

- Brain games—Sometimes one of the best ways to counter fatigue is to play tricks on the brain. This can be through simulating emergencies or trying something that requires as many senses as possible.
- Juice bar—While coffee or tea seem like obvious choices for providing a pick-me-up, a more natural way comes through drinking fresh-squeezed juices.
- Avoid heavy starches and proteins in your lunches. If you serve a meal of meatloaf, mashed potatoes, and apple pie, be prepared to roll out the mats and supply plenty of pillows. Instead, serve large salads with reasonable portions of fish or chicken and lots of nuts and berries—all energy-producing foods.
- Water—A well-hydrated body facilitates brain growth, whereas a dehydrated body forces the brain to kick into survival mode, taking precious brain cells away from your learning objective.
- Dance break—Studies have found that 80% of people know that dance improves their mood. And while 41% of the population feels like they dance poorly, they will still do it for the mood benefit if they aren't put in the spotlight.[5]

Those are just a few tools to keep in your arsenal, but the most important tactic to employ involves a mindset shift. We want to replace negative beliefs with positive beliefs. Here are some new beliefs you can convey about energy:

- Belief: The best things happen when I'm well rested.
- Feeling: I'm eager to discover the unexpected.
- Thinking: If I set boundaries and make good choices, I can accomplish more in less time.
- Relating: Meeting new people opens me to new possibilities.
- Action: I know how to manage my energy and will come ready.

In my experience, you can't just say these things and expect people to change their beliefs. The change will come through storytelling and experience.

As you prepare for the event, take time to share stories of attendees who managed their energy well and those who did not. Show the consequences of disregarding the Event Energy Law: "Those with the least energy will learn the least."

For example, in 2020, I found myself getting 3–4 hours of sleep per night before and during our conference. I drank copious amounts of coffee. I even avoided alcohol and heavy meals. But that's not sustainable.

I failed to compensate for the increased caffeine intake by increasing water consumption. My muscles began to cramp so that I couldn't stand or walk. Even worse, my brain began to cramp, and I made some poor decisions and said some very regrettable things. I'll never be able to undo the damage I did to a few of our volunteers through things I said in a burst of ten seconds. I feel deep regret for this, and I know it could have been avoided if I had been resting adequately. The problem was I drank so much caffeine that I couldn't sleep at night.

That might seem extreme for your guests, but I'm sure you have stories of guests who pushed their physical limits and received limited benefits from your event. Share these stories, and showcase opportunities you have for managing the energy flow.

You can also plan around the energy journey of your customers. We all know that after lunch is often a lull, so this is probably not the time to plan your most important content. Instead, do something that is highly interactive. Get people standing up and moving around. Provide stimulating conversation starters instead of long boring talks. Do something unconventional and unexpected.

Distraction

The human brain has changed profoundly in the last fifty years, especially due to the evolution of the digital world.[6] While we've made incredible technological strides, the vast majority of people are worse off by certain metrics. We are less able to concentrate for long periods of time, and we become much more easily distracted.

The very things we've created to make our lives better are actually making them more difficult at the same time. This is significantly relevant for events where we are inviting people to get away from their normal busyness to a place where they can have lingering conversations, entertain new paradigms, and do deep work on things that matter.

Okay, maybe your event doesn't promise all those deep aspirations, but I suspect you at least want people to get one big idea. But what if they never find it because they are distracted?

Here is a story of distraction. Have you ever been in a really good conversation to have it interrupted by a phone call, a social media notification, or a stranger? How does it make you feel?

A University of California study found that after each interruption, it takes over 23 minutes to refocus.[7] What's more, if the interruption takes you to something else, this multitasking can sap your brainpower—the equivalent of dropping 10 IQ points.[8]

In the summer of 2019, I took my daughter to see the touring performance of *Hamilton* in Oklahoma City. On the two-hour drive, we listened to the soundtrack nonstop. The hype outside the concert hall was palpable. People took selfies and lined up to buy merchandise. Once in our seats, the energy was unlike any Broadway show I've ever seen.

When the show started, it was electric. The performances were mesmerizing, the lights and sound creating the perfect experience, even though we were seated in the top balcony.

Then it happened. Midway through the first act, someone pulled out their phone and took a picture. The flash lit up the entire balcony. Fortunately, the performers didn't miss a beat, but I was distracted. I started an internal monologue: *Who does that person think they are? Can't they follow some simple rules? Where is the usher to take him (or her) out of here? How selfish to take a picture that won't even look good. I wonder if they'll try again.* The mental noise continued for several minutes before I could let it go.

The performance was so amazing that I was able to regain focus much faster than 23 minutes after that flash, but it took me at least five minutes. Unfortunately, at many events, when the state of focus is lost, so is the guest.

What are some of the things that cause distraction at events? I'm sure you'll add to my list, so this is merely meant to help you to identify the most significant sources of distraction that you should address for your next event:

- Notifications on mobile devices
- Emails from work or home
- Social media
- Failures with audio/visual technology
- Temperatures being too hot or cold
- Graphics or visual elements that don't support the experience
- Unfriendly staff or vendors
- Long lines
- Sessions that fill up
- Poorly planned transitions

Action: Discuss with your team the most likely sources of distraction. In addition to physical distractions, there are mental conversations your attendees engage in that need to be transformed if you want to move them from distraction to engagement. Here are some thoughts they might be having:

- Belief: I can't miss out on what's happening online.
- Feeling: I feel confused by all the competing messages in the event.
- Thinking: I've got too many thoughts, and I can't slow down to organize them.
- Relating: I'm unable to stay focused on one conversation because I might be missing another, more interesting one.
- Action: I'm constantly bombarded by messages pulling me away from the event.

Take them from distraction to engagement. Let me put your mind at ease. It's impossible to eliminate every distraction, and at some level, you need to trust your attendees to put themselves in a place to focus and stay engaged. Their intention to engage and stay present can help to overcome many of the potential problems you might have. Let's be honest: not all attendees have mastered these skills, but we can do some things to help.

Pete Vargas is the founder and CEO of Advance Your Reach. He brilliantly starts his events by acknowledging that we have things going on in our lives that might distract us. He does two things to counter that: First, he invites his attendees to send a thank-you video or note to someone who made it possible for them to attend the event. This subconsciously gives the attendee permission to fully engage in the event. But then he ups the stakes by addressing those who think they might not need to be at the event. He calls out the multitaskers and says something like, "Is it possible that there's something that might happen in the next two days that could change your business or life? You invested the time and money to be here. I challenge you to give yourself fully to this process. Those emails and text messages will still be there tonight."

I was the person he was calling out. I had come as a speaker. I had attended his event before and I didn't think I needed it. When he said that, I didn't feel guilty or ashamed. Instead, I felt invited to consider there might be more for me than I ever imagined. I distinctly remember two conversations that happened in the next few hours that changed the trajectory of my life.

Instead of asking people to just silence their phones, what if you were to invite people on a journey with you? If you're running a virtual event, ask your attendees to pack their bags as if they are traveling. We've created "Do Not Disturb" signs so the attendee can signal to their coworkers or family that they are attending an event. In some cases, it might be wise for an attendee to check in at a local hotel so they can truly focus.

Nobody likes being thrown off the merry-go-round when it goes too fast. Likewise, it's very boring when the ride seems like it's barely moving. It's worth evaluating your event to understand its weaknesses and the threats that could undermine your success. Your attendees, speakers, staff, and sponsors will all thank you!

Bread Bite

Question: Which element of DRIED presents the greatest threat to your event?
Exercise: On your own or with some of your team members, brainstorm at least ten ways to solve that problem. Don't evaluate the solutions until after

you have ten ideas on the table. Then narrow it down to one or two things you can do at your next event to minimize that problem.

Another Bite

If you want to dig deeper into this, utilize the matrices in Appendix B to help your team identify the beliefs, thoughts, or feelings that need to transform from negative to positive. It's a process that takes time and intentionality.

Section II:

Baking a Memorable Experience

Chapter 5:

THE ART AND SCIENCE OF CREATING A MEMORABLE EXPERIENCE

I'll never forget the smell of bread baking. My mother and grandmother both loved to bake bread. For a few years, my mother made so much bread that my preschool-aged son called her "Grandma Bread" instead of "Grandma Bev!" Now whenever I walk into a restaurant or a bakery where I can smell bread baking, I'm immediately taken back to happy times.

But I also remember taking a tour of a Wonder Bread bakery during grade school. I left feeling ill, but I couldn't figure out why for years. Now I know that I was smelling the artificial preservatives and all the powerful cleaners they used to keep the factory floors clean. I have an aversion for Wonder Bread to this day, and that association was marked by a smell.

The truth is, there are hundreds of restaurants and bakeries I've entered where I don't remember a thing. The bread was good, not great or terrible. The smells are appealing but not magical.

Events are very similar. They can evoke the same kinds of emotions. Some events create life-changing moments. Others spur revulsion while most leave us unchanged and unimpressed.

Why do you think that is? To get at the heart of it, let's start by analyzing how a master baker approaches his craft.

Baking Bread

I've spoken with several master bakers, and they all confirm that baking bread is really pretty simple: 1) Gather the ingredients; 2) mix them together; 3) allow the dough to rise; 4) shape the dough; 5) bake it; 6) eat it. Rinse. Repeat.

What could possibly go wrong? Before we answer that question, let's break it down just a little bit more.

The science of baking bread is really straightforward: get the measurement of your ingredients right, allow the dough to rise long enough, bake at the right temperature for the right amount of time, and you'll have an edible loaf of bread. Science will even help you understand how to measure your ingredients, how to fine-tune the rising, and even adjust the oven type and settings.

But at some point, the artist needs to kick in.

> "Baking bread can either be incredibly easy or very difficult. You can literally mix flour, yeast, salt, and water, and throw it in the oven, and you'll have a loaf of bread. But it will be forgettable. If you want it to be unforgettable, you need to focus on the technique, the quality of the ingredients, and time."
>
> —Baker Bettie

Choose your ingredients wisely. In terms of determining the flavor of your bread, the most important step is choosing your ingredients. The thing is, there really are only four primary ingredients: flour, water, salt, and yeast. Without those ingredients (and yes, yeast is optional; it's not added to unleavened bread), you cannot have bread. Yet the way those ingredients are combined, prepared, and baked can make dramatic differences in whether you have a generic loaf of sandwich bread or a beautiful artisan bread that makes your mouth water. You can add a special ingredient like raisins or spices, but those aren't necessary to make a great loaf of bread.

You could make the same case about events. Our primary ingredients are content, conversations, connections, and the choices we make about things like sound, lights, graphics, and so forth. It's how we choose these ingredients and mix them together that can cause our event to stand out or become just another boring event.

Focus on techniques. According to Baker Bettie, increasing the hydration level of the bread will allow for a much more complex flavor and interesting texture and crusts. However, this dough is more difficult to work with and new bakers struggle to get it right. The same can be said for event planners. New event organizers might become overwhelmed with too many moving parts and last-minute changes while the experienced organizer knows exactly which buttons and levers to push and pull.

Over the next few chapters, we'll discuss these different ingredients and how they affect the flavor of our event and the outcome we seek. But first, let's further explore the world of baking.

Meet Josh Allen. Josh Allen owns and runs Companion Bakery in St. Louis, Missouri. He primarily bakes bread for his customers: restaurants and caterers. He can spend months experimenting to get a loaf of bread to meet the customer's expectations for taste, texture, appearance, and feel. The questions Josh asks of his customers are very similar to how event planners think about creating amazing experiences.

Start with the end in mind. The first questions Josh asks his customers are "What do you want the bread to taste and feel like?" and "What's the experience you're looking for?"

This thoughtful intentionality is what separates average bakers from master bakers. The more specific you can get on the desired taste, feel, and experience, the easier it becomes to tell the story you desire.

Josh observed this can be very subjective, and it takes time to help a customer know what they really want. It often helps to compare other experiences. It's very important for the baker to suspend his own opinion and judgment because he's trying to create the perfect loaf for his customer, not what he wants.

> **Important:** All event organizers need to suspend their own opinions and preferences, too. In the early years of our event, I played jazz music with a live band as people walked in thinking this was perfect background music. It turns out that very few members of our audience loved jazz—and all five of them sat in the front row! When I began thinking about our audience and what they preferred to hear we changed our music choices and people responded very positively.

For instance, Josh had a sandwich shop looking for the perfect sandwich bun for a Poor Boy (a Cajun specialty). The bread needed to not only taste good but also complement the taste of the sandwich ingredients and hold together while the customer ate the sandwich. Coming out of the oven, the loaf might not look that different from a sub shop bun, but the texture, taste, and feel were customized for the exact experience desired. It took nearly a year to perfect the bun.

The same is true for great events. Cookie-cutter events can lose sight of the story they are seeking to tell. It's also easy to get lost in the minutiae of selecting venues, speakers, room setup, and logistics and forget the overall vision. Great event organizers ask lots of questions to determine the desired outcome.

For one conference I produced, we sought to select a party venue. Our team became enamored with the type of venue we might prefer for the party instead of thinking about the attendee and what their goal might be. That clouded our judgment and kept us from seeing that while a nightclub style venue might be affordable and easier to produce, it would not create a great place for free-flowing networking for a group of strangers who might primarily be men. Once we got clear on the experience, it helped us eliminate dozens of potential venues and get dialed in on the ones that would best support the story.

In another situation, we needed to trim the budget. It would be easy to look at large expenses and just cut them without regard for the effect on the experience. That's why the user experience must remain paramount. **You can get very creative in finding solutions when you're clear on the vision.**

Borrowing from Josh's experience in creating the perfect Poor Boy bun, here are the steps he takes, and we'll apply those at a high level to event production.

Customizing Your Event

There are four steps to customizing your event for your audience.

Step 1: Define the desired taste.

The flavor of the bread starts with the quality and quantity of ingredients. This takes tinkering to find the right amount and type of flour, salt, water, and yeast. The taste can be affected by other processes down the line, so Josh is meticulous to isolate changes along the way, knowing that the ingredients are the foundational starting place. While salt, water, and yeast have minimal effect on the taste, the type of flour can profoundly affect everything.

This is where you see the biggest differences between types of events. Depending on your goals, you might prefer a tradeshow, conference, workshop, retreat, or internal event. And get clear on whether your event is designed to teach, launch a product, facilitate networking, or fulfill continuing education requirements. Or is it some combination of these?

The following table provides an overview to help you think through the relative importance of five elements to decide what type of event you should create. The truth is that while there are categories of events, you need to create the best event for your audience. These categories do create certain expectations for your audience that you may or may not be aware of.

	Tradeshow	Conference	Workshop/ Seminar	Internal Event
Content	Low	High	High	High
Networking	Low	Medium	Medium	Low
Exhibitors	High	Medium	Low	Low
Parties	High	Medium	Medium	High—team building
Experiences/ Sightseeing	Medium	Low	Low	High

I spoke recently to a university professor who teaches as part of an event I attended a few years ago. I mentioned one of the instructors, and he bragged on her as his colleague. But then he asked me how her workshop was. I couldn't lie. I thought she had great content, but I was disappointed because it wasn't a workshop. It was just a lot of content delivery and then Q&A with her for the whole day. I expected time to work alone and in small groups, my expectation based on the label of "workshop."

My expectations were shaped by other events and how I would have approached the event. I'm not necessarily right or wrong, but the aggregation of the customer's expectations is something the event organizer must understand. My university professor friend admitted that the event provides no oversight to the instructors, so they can't control the quality.

Step 2: Allow for fermentation.

The difference between a commercial loaf of bread and an artisan loaf of bread comes down to intention and process. A commercial baker wants a very predictable outcome that can be created on an assembly line. To maximize output, bakers are forced to limit fermentation time.

> Note: Fermentation is one of the biggest differentiators between types and qualities of bread. For example, a French roll doesn't need to rise as much as a loaf of large sandwich bread.

There are three phases of fermentation.

Phase 1: The first phase of fermentation is the primary mix, when you combine the ingredients and create the dough. You might set the loaf aside for less than an hour if the bread doesn't need to rise too much or as much as several hours for loaves of bread needing more fluffiness.

Making use of naturally occurring yeasts in the air (as sourdough does) affects this process differently than if using baker's yeast. And all of this goes out the window if you're creating unleavened bread.

Have you ever seen a loaf of bread collapse in the oven? That's because the yeast was allowed to ferment too long before it got in the oven.

Unless you're doing a surprise event, most events require preparation so people can quickly enter in. The deeper the desire for networking or transformational work, the more important the pre-fermentation and fermentation are. I have found that 60 days is a good time to start building momentum toward an event, but it might be less depending on the scope and outcomes desired.

Phase 2: The second phase is for cutting and shaping the bread. The shape of a loaf affects how it will rise.

Imagine the difference between doing an event in a sterile warehouse and on a cruise ship. The "container" will dramatically affect many things about the experience. Some venues require you to create experiences. Others come with an inherent experience. You don't always get to control the venue, but be aware of how the venue affects the flavor of the event experience you're creating.

Phase 3: The final phase is called "oven spring." This is when you see the bread rising magically in the oven. When the bread reaches 140 degrees (F), it will stop rising. So the oven temperature has a significant impact on what the bread will turn out like. If you need bread to keep rising in the oven, keep the temperature lower. If you want the bread to develop a hard crust without a lot of rising, use a higher temperature.

If you're attending a Tony Robbins event, you'll notice they can start the show at full throttle because many people know what they signed up for and are ready before they ever arrive. The leaders can turn up the heat, so to speak. At events where no one knows each other and the topic is new, more time needs to be spent "warming up" the room.

When I attended a Savannah Bananas game, I noticed they were very intentional in the pregame show to get people used to participating. The DJ did all kinds of call responses and had people on their feet before the game ever started. He got the super fans stirred so they could bring others along. By the time the game started, it didn't take long for fans to be fully participating.

At some events, the "wave" is only halfheartedly joined, but at a Bananas event, it gets nearly 100% participation because people want to participate. It's all because the team knows how to turn up the heat at the right speed. It's part art and part science.

Variation

Andy Sharpe is CEO of Song Division. His company brings studio musicians to events to help attendees write and perform original songs about their event experience or a company initiative. The goal is to get people working together and tap into their creativity. You would expect this to be something that you would have to do after they've been together for a while (and maybe after they've had a drink). He agreed with this principle in general. But he said sometimes his company is invited to come to create a memorable, high participation experience at the very first session just to prime the pump and help people to drop their defenses.

It's all about intention. Why are you doing what you're doing? What if you spent a lot of time thinking about how quickly you're turning up the heat on your attendees?

In terms of the big goals of learning and connecting, let's think about how we prepare our attendees. For instance, if you're attracting a bunch of strangers to your event, it might be reasonable to assume they need time to feel comfortable being together before you ask them to get too vulnerable. If your event requires a lot of vulnerability, it's important to slowly turn up the heat on this.

If, however, your attendees are familiar with each other from online groups or they are coworkers, you can race past the warm-up activities and get straight into deeper material.

With the help of Tracy Nice, I've adapted the popular Invitation-Challenge model into the Invitation-Commitment matrix. The higher the level of invitation the lower the commitment and vice versa (see graph). Let's define these terms:

Invitation vs. Engagement

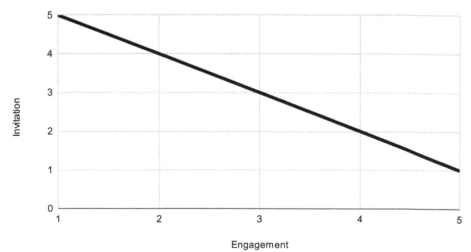

Invitation

The event organizer welcomes participation in some kind of activity. The more friction to participate, the higher the level of invitation. Our goal is to make it easy to say yes to participating and just show up. Examples of this might be a free breakfast before the event starts. It takes a little effort to go, and you might need a few reminders that it's happening, but there's no extra charge.

Commitment

The amount of commitment refers to the participation effort required from attendees. If a high level of engagement is demanded, then the invitation should be lower because you only want people to engage here who are ready.

Two clarifications: 1) You can use this model to think about the entire event. For instance, if your event retails for $5,000 that is a high commitment versus an event that runs $97. The attendees of these two different events have very different expectations, and you, as the organizer, can also have different levels of expectations of attendees at these events; 2) You can also use this model to assess various micro-invitation-commitment moments such as an opening party, lunchtime activity, or even content sessions.

Your ultimate goal is to help someone choose their own bagel. Have you ever been to a bakery that has dozens of types of bagels? It can become overwhelming.

I was speaking with one of the organizers of a 100,000-person event recently. With an event that large, it can become very overwhelming to choose your schedule. Their event guide is a 70-page book. One of their solutions is to create recommended paths for their top 8–10 avatars. This gives suggestions for someone to get started. Once they get moving and make a few connections, the event becomes an entirely different experience.

> **Warning:** If you're asking people to walk on coals (like Tony Robbins), you need a very strong invitation to get the high commitment required! Tony Robbins has something going for him that your event probably doesn't, and that's reputation. Many people have heard that they will be asked to walk on coals. They've watched the videos. Long before they signed up, they probably talked to people who've done it. It doesn't totally prepare them for the moment, but they probably paid for the event specifically because of that experience.

Here's a different example. If you're running a fundraising banquet, the event starts with high invitation and low commitment. You want people to get comfortable. Introduce them to people. Give them food and drinks. Make sure they enjoy themselves. Maybe have some fun games or even a raffle that doesn't require much investment. But the banquet will end with low invitation and high commitment. Not everyone is going to choose to accept substantial invitations in the mission of the fundraiser. Some people might even be invited to a more intimate gathering just for those able to make a significant investment.

The goal of most events is to move people to their next level of commitment. For some, that might be their first step. With others, it might be a very dramatic and significant step. Be careful not to judge. A small step for one person might be a huge step for another.

I remember getting into a bidding war with a parent of the private school I served in San Diego. We both wanted the honor of going to dinner with a famous author. I reached my upper limit very quickly since I worked on a pastor's salary. It was an amount I would have gladly spent on the meal, but I couldn't stretch beyond that. The parent against whom I was bidding was a good friend, and he bowed out, allowing me the honor of that meal. I learned later that he was willing to bid five or ten times more than I. My gift was a small commitment for him but a huge commitment for me. If he had bid $5 more, he would have won and maybe been celebrated by the school, but his commitment level would have been small.

Step 3: Shape the bread.

The shape of the bread is affected by the container and how it's molded. Obviously, the desired shape is determined by the look and use case for the bread. A hot dog bun definitely would be a challenge for a traditional hamburger.

While the oven is the event venue, and we'll get to that in a moment, the bread's shape is how you use that space. It includes room layouts, use of color, sound, lights, and the flow of the space. We'll dig into each of these areas, but they all affect the type of event you're creating.

Many artisan breads, like brioche, take bakers years to perfect. Bakers know not to ask a beginner to try some of these breads until they master certain skills. Likewise, don't expect that at your first event you'll be able to execute on all the amazing things you see events do that have been around for many years.

The X factor is time. How long you bake a loaf of bread affects many things. How long you spend planning for an event also dictates how ready you are. Allowing enough time in the schedule for breaks and transitions is super important.

But here's one you probably haven't thought of from longtime event planner, Elise Rollinson, CEO of Right Hand Events in San Diego:

> "The thing people forget to think about when picking a venue for an event is the load in and load out time and requirements. No, it's not the glamorous part, but it's often overlooked from both the customer and venue side. Missing the mark on this critical piece can cost extra money and even dictate what you are able to accomplish. Looking at the day of the week and time of day that setup and teardown will take place is very important, as after hours and weekend labor is often more expensive. I always recommend to plan a time buffer on either side, even if you can release it at a later date (which is definitely best practice as well)."

Step 4: Put it in the oven.

We started talking about this in previous phases, but the oven type, temperature, and conditions can make a massive difference in the outcome.

First, let's look at the type of oven. A pizza oven will create a different result than a traditional convection oven as will baking over an open flame. Artisan bakers will spend a lot of time studying the type of oven that will create the consistent eating experience they desire. Also, if the oven is part of your guest experience, that makes a difference

Jim Jonas, founder of Goat Milk Stuff, decided to build a pizza oven next to his pool so that he can create awesome experiences with family and friends around food and fun. He even lets his guests make and bake their own pizzas. It's all about the experience. But when his wife bakes bread to feed their staff of 30, she uses a large convection oven. That's about efficiency and consistency.

The oven is a metaphor for your event venue. If you decided to host your event at a baseball stadium, you might have a hard time doing a traditional conference with breakout sessions, but you could have fantastic stadium-style learning and massive parties or concerts. Likewise, an art museum might make an excellent choice for creative mixers and learning events that are highly hands-on and oriented toward small groups.

Next, let's look at how temperature affects not only how quickly the bread stops rising, but also the moistness of the bread and the crustiness. If you want to get a hard crust with a softer inside, you might choose a higher temperature for a shorter period of time in the oven.

Another factor is moisture. Many bakers will add moisture to the oven to create steam so that the bread stays moist, but in the case of the Poor Boy roll that Josh Allen created, he determined that the moisture was affecting the texture of the bread in unintended ways.

Are people coming to your event purely to learn? Do they care about networking and parties? The balance of content, networking, and fun should be addressed to your ideal customer. How you do these things is even more important.

In one of the first Social Media Marketing World conferences, an attendee kept complaining to our staff about everything from temperature to the length of breaks between the sessions, to room setups. Someone finally asked her some questions. She was a high-ranking engineer with NASA, and she came to learn as much as she could as fast as she could. She saw networking as fluff, and everything else we did to create space for marketers to connect and have conversations was worthless to her.

I would argue that our event wasn't designed for that engineer, but imagine if that was our core audience. We would want to change our venue, schedule, and vibe to accommodate the kind of learning event that would best serve her.

It's not hard to put on an event. It's much like teaching a 12-year-old to bake a loaf of bread. They'll be able to get the job done, and it will be edible. However, if you want to create a highly memorable and impactful event, it requires the skills of a master baker. The nuances required to move something from good to great take time and attention to detail.

Sometimes you need to hire a master event planner. Let me share an illustration from the world of biking.

When I was in college, a neighbor helped me to buy a Raleigh racing bicycle from the United Kingdom. It came unassembled, but I figured I'd been working on my bikes for years, so I could handle it. I put it together and tried to ride it, but something was off. I decided to take it to the local bicycle repair shop to get an expert opinion. That's when I heard the damning words, "Who put this together? My 12-year-old could have done better than this!" That's when I grew to respect the importance of experts and training.

Bread Bite

Just because something looks easy to do, doesn't mean it is.

Question: If you described your event as a loaf of bread, what type of bread would your attendees like? Are they expecting a loaf of Wonder bread or artisan bread? How does that compare to what you like at events?

Exercise:

1. Get your team together to bake some bread. Try a few different loaves, and be intentional about how you want each one to come out. Create a parallel between the choices you're making and the event you're planning. When you're done, see how well the results matched your expectations. If you have time, do this a couple of different times to see if you can improve your results. Every time you do this, make sure your intentions and expectations are clear so you can determine if the results matched your plans.

2. If you don't have a baker on your team (or someone you can hire to help you), go to a local bakery and talk to them about how they create experiences. See how they might go about planning an event.

Chapter 6:

GETTING YOUR CREW READY TO BAKE

I'll never forget Clark. He's a barista at my local Starbucks, and he wears a name badge decorated with a Superman theme. I picked up on this, and we started bantering about how "super" he is. Now, when I go to pick up my coffee, he always wants to know how to make my day super.

Let's stick with the restaurant metaphor for this chapter; after all, that's where we eat bread!

Restaurants are like events in that there is a pretty defined process to the customer experience that is inherent in every restaurant. For the sake of this chapter, think about restaurants where you are greeted by a hostess or a maitre d' and waited on by a server.

Think about the normal and extra steps involved with restaurant experiences:

1. You park your car (valet parking optional).
2. The outside door is opened for you by a greeter (optional).
3. The hostess greets and seats you.

4. Wait staff brings water and bread while you look at the menu.
5. Your server introduces herself and gets your drink order.
6. Drinks are served, and the server takes your food order.
7. Eventually your food is served.
8. Your server makes sure everything came out as expected. She fixes any problems and brings anything that is missing.
9. Your server keeps checking on you throughout the meal.
10. Dessert is ordered and served (optional).
11. Check is delivered and paid.
12. The hostess thanks you for coming as you leave.
13. You get your car (paying valet?) and leave.

With slight variations, almost all restaurants have some version of this service flow. What separates average restaurants from great restaurants? It's how these things are done and often by whom.

Think about one of your favorite restaurants and the reasons why you love it. It might be the food, the ambiance, or the entertainment, but I'll bet you notice that the staff are different. Great restaurants take care of their staff and thereby minimize turnover. But these restaurants also know how to empower the servers to create a great experience.

In Wichita, KS, where I live, there is a high-end steak restaurant called Chester's. The food and service are outstanding. Every server is highly invested in the experience and goes out of their way to make things happen that aren't on the menu and to provide extra value. On one visit, we had a particularly engaging server, and we ended up talking about his life and career. He made a deep impression on us. Imagine our surprise when he was our server at a different restaurant! I didn't immediately recognize him, but I noticed how he served us. Then I remembered.

In the world of events, our people are our greatest asset. The pandemic of 2020 forced events to reinvent themselves and get creative with how to create great experiences with limited budgets. Your staff and volunteers will make a memory.

Back to our baking analogy. I recently visited a local bread company expecting to be able to talk to a master baker because the place is known regionally for its bread. I was shocked when I spoke with her to learn that she really doesn't know that much. She just follows the instructions.

Contrast that with Josh Allen, whom we met in the last chapter, who is continuously seeking to create a great experience for his customers with every loaf he bakes. He fully understands every lever he can pull to modify the experience to make it perfect for each customer.

Do you want recipe followers or master bakers? That's a false dichotomy. Every master baker starts by learning to follow a recipe. But the great bakers start asking why and experimenting to see what happens. Truly great bakers do this with not just a desire to understand what's possible but also to solve a particular problem or create a specific outcome.

I'm a jazz saxophonist by training. I started learning notes and scales at a very young age. In seventh grade, I was introduced to the concept of improvisation. It scared me at first. I didn't want to play a wrong note. Slowly I learned a few things I could do safely. For a long time, that was how I approached jazz—I played safe notes. It wasn't until I started to study the masters by listening and mimicking them that my playing started to really take off. Over time, I've incorporated aspects of heroes like John Coltrane, Wayne Shorter, Stan Getz, Michael Brecker, Eric Marienthal, and Kirk Whalum.

How does that relate to your staff? You need to know your people and their roles. Some people need recipes. Some people are ready to mimic great mentors and move beyond just the recipe. Some are ready to lead on their own. Using a restaurant as an example, let's look at how this might affect a few roles using a simple matrix. This matrix could be useful for your team.

Role	Recipe	Mimic	Lead
Greeter	Follows a script	Models a head greeter	Trains other greeters
Server	Sticks to a very specific script	Follows one of the top-performing servers, and mimics what they do	Becomes a role model for all other servers
Cook	Sticks to the recipe religiously (In a restaurant, you really don't want your cooks changing the things on the menu.)	Watches to see where it's possible to incorporate some personal flair	Creates new dishes and concepts

One of my daughters was starting a new job at a restaurant. In her first week of serving, she had a large table that all showed up at different times. She has a spiel she uses before she takes everyone's order. It's pretty much a memorized script. Well since the party of eight arrived in five different cars, my daughter gave her spiel five times. She apologized to the first arrivers as they joined her in repeating her speech!

Where It Starts

I've visited dozens of Starbucks stores across the country. I like their nitro cold brew better than anywhere else's, and I'm somewhat addicted.

In visiting the stores, I've noticed that while the product is consistent, the experience is not. I asked a manager at a store in Wichita about this. She told me that it starts with the manager. The manager sets the tone. People will follow her lead. If she greets customers loudly, her staff will feel comfortable doing the same. If she remembers a customer's name and order, the staff will start doing the same. The little things being done over time make a huge difference in the culture.

I once interviewed Lee Cockerell, former COO for Disney Parks. He made a similar observation. He said the difference between Disney and other theme parks is the attention to detail and the constant desire to learn and improve. Employees are encouraged to find ways to improve the experience. For example, it was an employee who created the Fast Pass noticing that customers don't enjoy standing in line. But these employees wouldn't feel empowered if leadership didn't take the time to listen and respond to what they hear.

The right people in the right role

In his book *Good to Great*, Jim Collins built the case that it's important to get the right people on the bus before you worry about what they do. Are they a good culture fit? If they are volunteering, do their motives align with your needs?

In the early years of Social Media Marketing World, we didn't have a lot of experience with volunteers and didn't understand this principle. So, when a friend of the company approached us about volunteering, we were immediately impressed. This person had extensive experience in television production, and we knew we needed those skills in helping us create a great keynote stage experience.

But while she had the right experience, she had a personal conflict she didn't reveal. Due to life circumstances, she couldn't just walk away from her business for the three days of our conference to serve our event. When she signed up, she said she could. But she didn't tell us about the change, and we were left in a bind when she didn't show up for meetings or assigned shifts. We eventually had to proceed without her, but it taught us the importance of being sure you have the right person.

We had another volunteer who passed all of our application processes with flying colors. But it turned out that while he was an amazing connector, he had a personal ambition to use that position to get close to the speakers so he could interview them. When he started doing it while he was on shift, we had to confront him and ask him to wait until he was off duty.

These aren't bad people. They just had different objectives and goals. Sometimes we can work with those constraints and find a role that works. Other times, we've had to say, "You know, it seems based on your goals that you would be better served to attend the event as a paying customer."

Power

In this section, we'll talk about the power of different elements that go into creating your events.

The Power of Preparation and Practice

The first few years of doing events were exciting. We were growing steadily and getting praise. In fact, the compliments were so strong that we didn't see a problem we were creating. We had dozens of people who wanted to work for us, and our team needed to grow. What did we do? We hired people who loved us and who had skills that filled certain programmatic needs we had. But what we didn't know was that just because someone is good at a desk job, that doesn't mean they will thrive on-site.

There are several facets of this that are worth exploring as you build your team.

#1: Hire the right temperament. When you're small, you don't have the luxury of hiring lots of different people, so you need people with the right skills and the temperament to handle the pressure of events. Being an event planner is one of the five most stressful jobs anywhere according to Career-Cast.[9] We create a picture of a duck or swan in our minds. Can this person paddle furiously underwater while showing a calm, pleasant demeanor to the public? How do they respond to change, multiple demands, and time-sensitive deadlines (e.g., everything needs to be done *now*)?

#2: Create clarity about on-site roles. One of our mistakes was that we didn't think through carefully enough what someone's role would be on-site. For example, I recently met with our customer service manager and discovered that her role was very defined on-site for the first day of the event, but after that, she kind of floated wherever needed and was put in roles that were less than ideal for her skills. Our plan moving forward is to look at what each person is doing every hour of the event so that we create reasonable expectations and clarity.

#3: Provide training for the on-site role. Many times, you'll be asking staff to do things during the event that aren't part of their daily job description. Be sure you provide at least the same level of training for staff as you do for volunteers, but I would encourage you to provide more. Volunteers look at staff as the experts. They won't know that Sally from editorial doesn't work on the event throughout the year. Give her some extra preparation so she can help the volunteers. Besides, Sally wants to do her work with excellence, and a little bit of preparation will help.

While we're talking about training, let's talk about volunteers. One of the things people love about our event is we actually spend time training them. Our alumni volunteers get tired of hearing the same things every year, so we've discovered some ways to solve this with technology. We now create online training courses that people can take at their own pace so that we can use our on-site training time to provide inspiration, reminders, and primarily practice the things that they can't really do at home. You can use any number of training programs like Kijabi, Learndash, or Thinkific.

#4: Practice, practice, practice. Athletes and musicians know this mantra, "How we practice is how we'll perform." The problem for most event staff is they *never* practice what they will do on-site, so they are constantly caught off guard. Let me give you some examples from my experience.

Our event venue is approximately one-third of a mile from end to end. That means the events team usually puts in 20,000 to 40,000 steps each day. I work from home and normally take anywhere from 2,000 to 8,000 steps daily. In 2020, I knew this was a problem, so I worked myself up to 10,000 steps daily right before the event. It was too little too late. I had major problems with connective tissue in my legs (called iliotibial tract bands (a.k.a. IT bands)) that made it so I couldn't walk or even stand. I had to miss one of our parties because I was in so much pain that I spent the evening doing yoga and in the jacuzzi trying to relax my tissues so I could sleep and put in another day. If I had spent longer preparing my body, that wouldn't have happened.

There are many predictable things that happen during your event. For instance, it's pretty much guaranteed that something will go wrong with your audio/visual technology. This likely isn't the fault of your A/V company. Equipment fails, and good A/V companies will bring backups because they know it may happen. For example, a microphone will fail or the sound system won't work, or a video won't play in a speaker's slide deck. Instead of being surprised by these known potential problems, spend time roleplaying how you'll handle it with your team.

Here are some scenarios you can practice. Rehearse how you'll respond to each. Come up with your own scenarios:

1. Long lines develop at the coffee break, lunch, or the bathrooms.
2. A customer complains about the temperature in the rooms.
3. A volunteer starts complaining and griping about the role they're in and spreading gossip about your team.
4. An attendee decides to sneak into your keynote room and place promotional items on 500 seats.

Yes, that last one has happened multiple times. My favorite was the year that they somehow wheeled in hundreds of bottles of salt with a message for a multilevel marketing program and put them on all the chairs in the first five rows. Our team felt a-salted (dad joke).

#5: Visualization can be just as good as practice. The science of neuroplasticity has shown the power of visualization to be just as good as real practice for many things. If you have a remote workforce, as many companies do, it's possible to guide people through exercises where they see themselves performing in different roles and scenarios and how they want to practice. If athletes and musicians can do this to accelerate their preparation, event athletes can, too (we are actually part athlete, part artist, and part superhero)!

How might this work? Here are two ways I use visualization. First, get the team together with the event schedule. This can be done on a video call. Have someone call out the show hour by hour. Each person should then say where they are at the moment mentioned, and then close their eyes and visualize themselves doing what they were assigned to do. This exercise helps to identify stressful parts of the agenda as well as reveal any problems where someone is expected to do three things at once.

The second way is a much deeper, more personalized exercise. In this scenario, you provide team members with multiple scenarios where they can visualize themselves at work. As we discussed before, create problem scenarios. They can practice in their mind's eye how they will respond. To enhance this, encourage staff to find places in their community where something similar might happen. Tell them to go observe how others do it, then visualize how they would handle the same situation. For instance, restaurants deal with customer service issues every day, so you might encourage staff to go to a busy restaurant and primarily sit and observe. They should make notes on what they liked and what they would improve. Then they can take both lists and visualize themselves doing the same thing.

The power of belonging

I recently found myself wondering why we prefer certain restaurants over others. You see, I recently asked my online community for recommendations on restaurants with a great customer service experience, but the answers I received almost exclusively talked about the food, venue, and vibe. Only when I pressed did people talk about customer service. Service is something you only notice when it's really good or really bad.

When I arrived at Starbucks this morning, Winn greeted me from the drive-thru window as I drove by. Clark greeted me loudly as I walked through the door, and another barista asked me if I wanted the usual. They made me feel like I belong.

I'll never forget the only time I ever ate at a Ritz-Carlton. It seems like it was yesterday, but it's actually been nearly twenty years. I was meeting the manager, so, unbeknownst to me, he let his staff know I was coming.

Numerous people greeted me, starting with the valets.

I felt like a fish out of water. I'm not used to eating with three forks and linen napkins. I'm pretty sure I made a mess and was an embarrassment to my friend, the manager.

But nobody made me feel like I didn't belong—quite the opposite. Everyone went out of their way to make me feel special.

That's what great service is ultimately about. It's taking care of the guests' needs to make them feel special and important.

The power of greetings

Greetings make a huge difference in customer experience. This hit home this morning at my local Starbucks. I was trying to decide whether to go through the drive-thru, order by mobile, or just go inside.

When I saw how long the drive-thru line was, I decided against that option. Since I was already there, I decided to go inside. I've become acquainted with a few of the staff over the last several years.

As soon as I opened the door, Jharon, the manager, greeted me enthusiastically. She pulled me aside and asked about my family and conference. Because she wanted to keep talking to me, she asked me to step aside while she took another order. We kept talking even though she was very busy.

And then she brought me my coffee personally. "Here you go, Mr. Phil."

What you don't know is that it had been two or three months since my previous visit, and I've only spoken with Jharon three times and never at length.

I will always go inside at that Starbucks because they know my name and it's worth the extra five minutes to be seen.

In watching Jharon work, I noticed that she's built that same kind of rapport with several customers. Her staff follows her lead. It's become a different experience from when the previous manager worked there (and she was good, too).

At events I lead, I ask our staff to work hard to place friendly/familiar faces at the doors to make people feel welcome. As much as possible we use their names because we know that hearing our name is like the best song we've ever heard (unless, of course, we're being scolded by our mother—Philip James Mershon, you get down here. . . still makes me cringe).

The power of attention to detail

I recently was making a protein shake, and I discovered after tasting it that I had misread the recipe. I included two tablespoons of the mix instead of two teaspoons. That made a profound difference, all because I didn't look carefully enough. I could make excuses about my weakening eyes and not seeing the difference between Tsp and Tbsp, but it doesn't matter. Sometimes these details can be fatal and not just an annoyance.

At a fastmoving event, it's easy to overlook details when the show must proceed. That's why detailed checklists are so important and helpful—until you forget to review them.

For one event I led, our team had a fair amount of turnover, and some members of the new team thought the checklists we used felt a bit restrictive and unnecessary, so we didn't review them. Let's just say that will never happen again. Those lists would have saved us many little problems—things most users would have never noticed, but it would have prevented many gray hairs and more premature baldness.

The power of presence

Your staff's impact on your event is disproportionate to their size. The way your crew shows up at each stage of the event is felt and seen. If your staff can't wait to start packing up the event, attendees notice. If your staff is bored, irritated, or tired, attendees pick up on these clues and start to disengage or distance themselves.

Have you ever been to a restaurant where the waitresses complain and gripe behind the scenes, but they don't realize you can hear them? It can be very awkward. When I go to these places, I try to leave as quickly as possible and vow to never return because I don't feel valued. I don't want to hear their gripes unless there's something I can do about it.

Since you're reading this book, I'm assuming you're a leader. Leaders set the tone for the rest of the team. You should be one of the first to arrive and among the last to leave. You can go out of your way to value the team while also paying attention to your customers, speakers, and vendors. Obviously you're not omnipresent or omniscient, but its important to keep tabs on all the players at your event.

The Perfect Meal

In the movie, *Babette's Feast*, a sect of austere Danish Christians lived in suspicion of all outsiders and anything filled with pleasure. Babette came to live with them to seek refuge from violence in Paris. It took her 14 years to earn the trust of the community. Then one day, she won the lottery. Instead of spending all the money on herself, she decided to prepare a lavish meal for her friends. The rich food prepared with love slowly broke down walls, and the community learned to enjoy food, life, and each other.

Most of us aren't leading events for people who dislike us or each other, but I would venture to say an event prepared with attention to detail and served with the same love will create a sense of belonging that will open the doors for all kinds of transformational moments. It starts with getting to know your customers and anticipating their needs.

I shared a meal with friends while conducting some business. At one point, I retold a story that powerfully touched me. In fact, I can't tell the story without crying, and that time was no different. Our waitress noticed my crying and quickly came up, grabbed my empty glass, said, "You need another drink," and went to get it. It led to a humorous conversation, and she got a bigger tip than normal all because she created a moment for us. I had to pay for the extra drink—I guess I did kind of ask for it.

Vendors are crew, too. Your event guests can't tell the difference between your core staff, volunteers, and vendors. Especially if you ask the vendors to wear your staff T-shirts, as we do. But many times, vendors have different core values than you do. How do you overcome this?

We invite all of our vendors to our orientation training, but here's the deal. You can't change someone's operating system in an hour. Whereas we can select the right people as staff and volunteers, we have to live with the vendors' team members. We do make it known that we are looking for friendly, customer-centric team members, but we've noticed that doesn't mean the same things to everyone.

For instance, I would venture to say most fast-food restaurants understand the importance of customer service. But there is a vast difference between Chick-fil-A and McDonald's in most settings. Chick-Fil-A prioritizes service in their training and modeling. McDonald's might include this in their training, but they seem to be even more concerned about efficiency and consistency.

Bread Bite

Question: How can you make sure you have a good culture fit with the right people doing the right things?

Exercise: Go with your team to a restaurant that has a reputation for great service. Make a list of everything they do that impresses you. Write down the lessons you can learn. If you really want to have a fun, go to a restaurant where they are known for poor service. Contrast the two experiences.

Bonus: Review your staff selection and training process to cultivate great customer service.

Chapter 7:

YOUR MAIN INGREDIENT: CONTENT THAT PRODUCES DOUGH

I'll never forget Ken. He was selected to speak for a leading industry event on two topics I love: music and marketing. I read his description and got super excited. I thought to myself, *Finally, someone gets me.* Unfortunately, I couldn't have been more disappointed. I left the session early as his well-written session description didn't match his material and his delivery fell flat. In retrospect, I suspect he convinced the event organizers to give him a chance based on that title, description, and a short demo. Have you had this happen?

I'm making an assumption by this point in the book: you're designing an event that is content-rich. Trade shows, expos, and pure networking events are going to look different even though some of these principles apply.

To keep our baking image going, people who attend a content-heavy event are probably not looking for a Wonder Bread experience. There's nothing wrong with store-bought bread—it's perfect for making a PB&J sandwich to take for lunch or some quick sustenance. But if you're looking for a transformational experience in your business or life, you're looking for something a little extra or different.

A baker knows that the first thing she should change to affect the taste of a loaf of bread is the quality of the flour. Instead of getting "run of the mill" flour—which means B grade or ordinary—bakers will look for unique ways to mill the grain, perhaps even getting a custom run just for them. They might be looking for specialty grains with a specific taste profile, or an organic or gluten-free grain.

Have you noticed that in the early days of gluten-free products, most of the gluten-free bread options weren't very good? Now bakers have found ways to deliver great-tasting bread that actually holds together.

That's what you need to do for your audience. Get to know their unique tastes and preferences so you can bake the perfect loaf of bread for that audience. It requires experimenting and refining. Every audience will be slightly different.

Your Goal

Here's your goal: **"To produce the right content that leads to meaningful conversations so you can set the stage for the conversion you seek."**

That sentence would have bothered me in my early days. I didn't think I was looking for a conversion—that sounded too salesy. I merely wanted people to gather, learn some good stuff, and come back. Oh, and tell their friends.

Think about this: coming back and sharing the experience is a form of conversion.

You might have a more defined conversion you seek, such as buying a more expensive program, deepening their relationship with you, or making some kind of personal commitment. It all starts with the content journey. That means it starts with your customer.

Your Customer

I was sharing ideas about an upcoming event with my team, and someone naturally asked the question, "Who is our customer avatar?" The truth is, we didn't know at that point in time. We needed more data.

That's true for you too. How well do you know your customers' preferences, interests, and demographics?

If you're planning an event for a millennial man, it's going to be quite different from an event for a middle-aged woman. A predominantly North American event will feel quite different from a European event, even if it's still in English. The choices you make about speakers, decorations, seating, parties, entertainment, and even forms of content will be different.

I remember the first time I went to one of our competitor's events and thought to myself, *They're doing it all wrong.* But I didn't realize that their audience was significantly different from ours. They were attracting male internet marketers who owned their own businesses. We were attracting female social media marketers who worked for someone else. They are part of the same broad market of digital marketing, but as that industry matured, we grew to understand that the learning needs and the type of experience desired will be significantly shaped by that audience.

The same is true for bakers. If you know your audience will be happy with a prepackaged loaf of bread, don't spend time crafting an artisan loaf of bread. But I will venture to say that everyone loves a good homemade loaf of bread for the right occasion. Just don't ask someone to make a PB&J on a hard-crusted French roll—it can be done, but it's a crumby experience (pun intended)!

Did you ever have to remove the crust from the bread so your kids would eat the sandwich? If you put the wrong crust on the bread, everyone will start to remove the crust. You will not only have a mess, but everyone will feel frustrated.

That's what it's like when you miss the mark on your content. If people are having to work too hard to find the sessions that really help them, they will get frustrated and leave. And they may never tell you why or even fully understand why themselves. They just know something's off.

That's why it's very important to take your time to get to know the tastes and preferences of your audience. Good bakers do taste tests. Good event planners run surveys and focus groups.

Choosing the Right Content

Start with your audience. There are many ways available to see what your audience cares about, and it doesn't necessarily require the expensive focus groups of yesterday. Social media is one of the best "free" focus groups available. If you ask the right questions of the right people, you can get incredible insights.

Social media: your modern focus group

The best way to do this is to have a hypothesis that you're testing. On social media, people typically won't respond if it requires them more than 10 seconds to come up with an answer to your question. Keep it simple and easy to respond to.

One year, we had fun with this as we tried to decide what color of carpet we should use. You might be trying to decide whether people prefer cocktails or beer, or karaoke versus quiet networking.

Here are some great ways to start your questions:

- Would you rather. . . then put two ideas against each other.
  - Example: "Would you rather stay up for a late-night networking party or go for an early morning networking walk?"
- How would you respond to this statement? Insert a statement that will evoke a response.
  - Example: "Free coffee should be available at all conferences."
- Am I the only one? This also gets people to either side with or against you.
  - Example: "Am I the only one who hates forced networking events?"
- Here's an unpopular opinion. . . Now you're getting people to take a side and see who agrees with how you're viewing things.
  - Example: "Here's an unpopular opinion: I think speakers should save their Q&A sessions for the hallway since most of the questions asked aren't relevant to the majority of us in the room."
- Don't you hate it when. . . insert a pet peeve you think your audience has and see if they resonate.
  - Example: "Don't you hate it when you get to an event, get checked in, and then find you have no idea where to go or what to do? It's as awkward as walking into the middle school lunch room and not knowing who to sit with."

Surveys can take it deeper. Sometimes you need more profound and more precise insights. That's when a survey of your audience can help. Be sure to ask enough qualifying questions so you can segment the audience that matches the people you hope to attract to your audience.

What if you haven't built that audience yet? Borrow the audiences of other people. Perhaps you can partner with people who have the audience you hope to attract and invite them to poll their audience with you. Just be sure to share the results of the survey with those partners.

Talk to your customers. If you need even deeper insight to ensure you're hitting the target, get on the phone with some of your customers. There is nothing better than hearing straight from customers. Try to record those calls so you can transcribe the actual words they use and not the way you heard them.

Confirmation bias is your worst enemy. If you think you know what your audience wants and needs, everything you read and hear will confirm that opinion. That's why Josh Allen of Companion Bakery said the first job of a baker is to set aside his subjective opinions to be able to truly understand the palate of his customer. The same is true for event organizers.

Martin Fretwell is a longtime event industry veteran. At one point in his journey, he decided to interview 100 of his best customers to understand their needs. Most of these people hold executive-level jobs. His discoveries led to an unexpected change in his career as he grew to understand the client's greatest need wasn't more content but more meaningful networking. He wouldn't have gained that insight without listening to his customers. Before listening, his improvements had a minor effect on his satisfaction scores, but once he shifted the focus, the scores improved dramatically.

What's the lesson? Listen to your customers. How well do you know them? Be sure you're planning the event for them and not for yourself.

All this feedback should help you identify what your audience wants to learn and how they like to learn. Some people prefer to learn through conversations. Others prefer to absorb lots of information. Still others learn best through hands-on demonstrations. The subject matter and your audience will help you decide what works best.

Thinking Ahead

The future of learning is changing. Technologies like virtual reality are starting to make things possible in learning communities that were never before imagined. I spoke recently with an executive from General Electric who installed virtual reality learning centers on location with all of their medical device customers who were spending $1 million or more so that they could do remote learning. She told me it has transformed the lives of her support team members. They no longer have to spend 15–20 days per month on the road. And the customers love it because they can train their team much more quickly and thoroughly without taking the device offline for training days.

Find the right speakers. There are many ways to find speakers for your event. All have validity. The ones you choose will be dictated by how connected you already are with experts in your industry and how much control you want over the content experience.

Some events will have a "call for speakers," where anyone can submit an application and there's a review team that chooses which ones fit that year's agenda. This allows for lots of diversity and gives room for newcomers to find your stage. But it's also riskier. People can look really good in an application or on a sizzle reel.

I remember cringing through a session at a conference one year. The speaker had a novel idea, and I could see why it was attractive to the event organizers. But he didn't deliver on his promise, and the organizers had no way of knowing that he couldn't back up his 3-minute pitch with a great 45-minute presentation. It was an eyeopener for me because I probably would have picked that session, too.

A different approach is to hand recruit every speaker. This takes time to build relationships and do lots of networking and vetting. But it ensures a higher-quality program. The danger is you can settle for inviting your friends and not find new talent unless you're constantly searching for new talent.

If you're willing to pay for speakers, look at speakers bureaus. They can help you find quality presenters who can deliver on your goals. If one of your values is to find speakers who will become part of your event community, be sure to negotiate this into the contract. I've discovered many attendees who complain that they wanted to talk with a speaker who showed up at the last minute, gave their talk, and left as soon as they were done. It might be cool to say you had Serena Williams speak at your event, but your audience might prefer to be able to speak with the presenter rather than watch them disappear the moment they step offstage. Consider asking speakers to invest at least one day in your event.

Many events combine all these approaches to find the right mix of speakers. I think the types of speakers you want are even more important than where you find them. Here are some things to consider. Your event will value some of these more than others.

Look for speakers who embody these characteristics:

- Go-givers: Are the speakers coming to serve your community, or are they coming to sell their books and services?
- Community members: Are your speakers coming to be part of your event, or did they come just to give their talk and leave? We ask our speakers to stay for at least a full day.
- Adaptable: Are the speakers willing to customize their material for your audience, or are they coming to give their canned talk?
- Flexible: Can the speaker adjust their materials to your audio/visual constraints?
- Humble: Does the speaker come across as a demanding diva or an eager partner?
- Students: Do your speakers get to know your audience and understand how your audience is different from other places they speak?

One of my favorite stories comes from a leading speaker in our industry. I'll leave out his name so as to not embarrass him. In 2019, this speaker was one of our top rated speakers. We were excited to invite him back in 2020 but shocked when he became one of our two lowest-rated speakers. I frankly had never seen such a dramatic decline. To his credit, when I shared that feedback, he immediately reached out to apologize. We got on a call. Through the course of our conversation, he realized that he completely misread our audience and gave a talk that worked well for other events but didn't serve the needs of our community.

Based on his response and continued industry leadership, we decided to give him another shot in 2022. He completely flipped it back around and returned to a top 10 position. He spent a long time studying the needs of our audience and gave a talk just for them. The audience gave him rave reviews.

That's the kind of speaker you want!

> **Side note:** It's worth giving second chances. People do change and grow and sometimes very quickly. I can think of another speaker who performed poorly in our online events. I was concerned to bring her to our conference even though she does well on camera. Other members of the team felt like she deserved a chance. I'm glad they prevailed, as she was also a highly rated speaker and it turns out she shines on stage whereas the online experience doesn't reveal her true brilliance.

Conversations and Conversions

The result of great sessions should be action. That action can look different depending on the audience, subject, and goals. But in most cases, I expect to see conversations arising from great sessions. In fact, really good sessions get those conversations started before it's even over.

The **external processors** (people who internalize information by talking) need permission and space to have those conversations pretty immediately. The **internal processors** (those who need time and space to quietly ponder what they've heard) also need time and space to have internal conversations before they are ready to talk.

Plan space and time the activities to serve both audiences. One of the choices I've made is to increase the break time between sessions to allow time for three types of conversations:

1. Q&A with speakers
2. Conversations with your neighbor or a group of people with similar interests
3. Space and permission for internal processing

I'm an internal processor. If you give me even five minutes to quietly process, I will be far more likely to engage with the external processors. The emcee can set the tone for this.

Let's talk about conversions for a minute. If your event is designed to get people to upgrade to a premium product, that is your primary measure of success. But I would argue that before you ever get there, you need to create a number of micro-conversions along the way. You have to get people to show up and choose to stay present. You invite participants to join small-group exercises. You challenge attendees to try various experiences you've created. You offer opportunities for free consulting with your team where they might be exposed to your offer, but you also provide incredible value.

If you're not selling something, you still have most of these conversions taking place. No matter what type of event you hold, you're looking for someone to keep showing up and find so much value that they want to come back and bring their friends. Retention is a huge sign of success for experience-driven events.

Brick and mortar

Do you remember the story of the Three Little Pigs? Imagine that the third pig built his house out of bricks but forgot to use mortar to hold it together. The Big Bad Wolf would have still been able to knock it down. Bricks are better than sticks, but they only work when they are cemented together.

Too many events are like a brick wall without mortar. There are beautiful, ornate bricks, but nothing is holding them together. People come to see the bricks. In general, they don't care what kind of mortar you use, but the mortar connects things.

What is mortar at events? Everything that happens between sessions. It's your emcees, entertainment, activations, snacks, coffee, lunch, and conversation opportunities. This is the time when people are most likely to check out mentally or physically from your event. But if you are highly thoughtful about how you create the connectedness between sessions, you can greatly increase the sense of immersion and community for your attendees.

In my opinion, this starts with your emcees. How well are they monitoring the emotions in your room? How well are they getting your audience talking with each other?

Jon Berghoff, CEO of XChange, is a master at doing this. He starts his events by playing with the house band and getting people on their feet singing and dancing songs designed to put people in the right frame of mind for the event. He models the mindset and behavior he desires from attendees and then leads them into conversations that he weaves between presentations and personal and small-group work. He's like a conductor. Jon moves people through various experiences that are all designed to help people learn, internalize, and apply the concepts presented.

Content Format

When you understand your audience, you will get dialed in to the learning format that serves their needs best. This is driven by the learning objectives, learning styles, and presentation styles of your presenters.

Learning objectives

What are you hoping will happen at your event? How do various sessions help accomplish that larger goal?

There are five basic types of content delivery:

- **Keynote sessions** are meant to teach you a new way to think.
- **Breakout sessions** are designed to teach you how to do something.
- **Workshops** give you a chance to try a new skill or process.
- **Conversational sessions** spark discussion on things presented at the event or of interest to the community. These could be a precursor to a session or as a follow-up. For some audiences, the real learning happens in the conversations. Don't discount this.
- **Product demo or sales presentation.** These are usually paid opportunities from vendors who have a product or service that might be interesting to your audience.

If these are your five types of content, how are you deciding on the right mix? Keep in mind that one session can only successfully introduce one major shift in thinking, behavior, or skill. Most people coming to your event will at most embrace two or three major shifts during the event. Embracing even just one shift can be considered a success.

Learning style

I'm going to state something undeniable: Adults learn differently from children. But it's not as different as you might think.

Children learn by stacking new ideas on existing ideas they understand. So do adults.

Children learn best when all their senses are engaged (sight, sound, and touch especially). So do adults.

Children learn through four primary modes and some are easier than others based on developmental stage, personality, and other factors. Those modes have been called learning styles, but most of the current literature debunks this as something to overly focus on. But we actually do learn through these modes, and a great event includes opportunities for all four. Adults still have learning preferences.

What are the four learning preferences or modes?

- **Visual learning** happens through watching and observing.
- **Auditory learning** happens through active listening.
- **Kinesthetic learning** happens through active participation, where learners try out new tools, ideas, or methods.
- **Reading and writing** is what you're doing right now, at least, if you're taking notes. At events, this might happen where a session leader asks people to read a paper and then discuss it. Or perhaps, people are asked to read some material in advance that will be reviewed and amplified during the event.

While these learning modes shouldn't dominate the way we prepare our learning experiences, they do show the need for a variety of content-delivery methods. For example, we know that people learn better when we combine visual and auditory learning. The retention increases dramatically when we also give people a chance to try something we've been teaching.

If you want to hit the majority of your learners, combine visual and auditory styles. This works because 65% of learners are visual learners (perhaps why video is doing so well these days) and 30% are auditory (podcasts and audiobooks work great for these learners). Only 5% of learners are kinesthetic. All types of learners can glean from and enjoy stories.

Experience Profiles

Naomi Clare Crellin is founder and CEO of Storycraft Lab, the creator of the Experience Profiles.[10] These profiles arose from a desire to enhance personalization at events and help event designers understand their audience's behavioral preferences based on well-documented academic frameworks. These frameworks help us understand social, interpretive, learning, and leadership preferences. What resulted is a set of six experience profiles which help organizers ensure their create a more inclusive event and promote dialogue about adjustments needed to match the unique makeup of every event.

Storytelling

Entire books have been written on the power of storytelling. In fact, this is the primary way we received our oral history for generations. Humans love a good story and are far more likely to remember a story than a principle.

This truth bothers many of my speaker and pastor friends. We spend a lot of time formulating really cool methods and theories, but when people leave, they are likely to only remember one or two concepts and some stories.

I remember one of my first sermons out of seminary. I created this cool 3x3 matrix that featured all of the principles from the sermon that I shared with the congregation. I printed it up and handed it out for them to follow as I preached. Afterward, the comments were along these lines, "That was interesting, Pastor, but I don't remember anything you just said." When I preached the same sermon to become an ordained minister, the committee asked me if I really preached that sermon. They felt like it was academically interesting, but not very helpful to people.

I needed more stories and less theory. Most speakers are the same, depending on their topic.

Tamsen Webster trains speakers to approach their Tedx talks as master storytellers. She challenges us to invite our audience into the story by making them the hero of the story. Introduce early the challenge and the threat (the antagonist). Provide some early success, but then deepen the pain by introducing more failure. At this point, the guru comes on the scene showing the way to a new path of escape. The guru might be our unique solution or method.

People are used to this storytelling method and will find themselves drawn in if you include them in the narrative.

To implement this idea, Michael Port, CEO of Heroic Public Speaking, suggests using Aristotle's three-act structure to sculpt it. Most plays, movies, and TV series, as well as almost any story and many jokes use the three-act structure.

Three-Act Structure

Here's how the three-act storytelling structure works:

Act 1 is the context. It sets up the place, time, and setting. It reveals what you need to know in order to understand what's about to happen. If that exposition becomes too lengthy or nonspecific, the listener will likely check out. If, on the other hand, you don't provide enough detail, the listener might get confused by the second act, and then check out. You need to provide just enough details for the audience to understand the rest of the story.

Act 2 is the conflict. This is where an inciting incident happens, something that creates conflict. Normally, when a conflict occurs, some action follows. Then that action provokes another conflict, which often produces more action. Basically, the story keeps building tension through conflict and action. It's all rising toward Act 3.

In a great story, the protagonist is on a mission to get what they want but is thwarted by the hurdles, boundaries, and roadblocks that get in their way. There is often an antagonist who blocks the path toward victory. The protagonist keeps trying to overcome all these roadblocks but keeps failing. The more tension, the better the story.

Act 3 is the resolution. The people in the story lived happily ever after, everyone died in the end or, if it's a joke, it's the big punchline. The resolution (or payoff) has to be worth the exposition and all of the conflict. Normally the resolution involves the intervention of some expert or guide who shows the protagonist the way of escape, or fights with or for the protagonist.

Try putting your stories through this simple framework. If you want a more complicated formula, use the one found in *Save the Cat* by Blake Snyder. Blake is a Hollywood screenwriter who walks through the building blocks of all the Hollywood Blockbuster movies.

Content-delivery skills

Most events that I work around assume that the speakers coming to them have decent delivery skills. If you're paying someone, you certainly expect the speaker to be a professional. If they are hand-selected or picked from an application, you might be able to suggest coaching, but you'll have to decide whether you want to offer that or just create a resource that has suggestions.

Here are some areas speakers often need help:

- Slide preparation—many new speakers have too many slides with too much information on the slides. Remember the simple adage: less is more.
- Stage presence—does the speaker make good eye contact? Do they make good use of the stage and engage all parts of the room, including the online audience? Are they purposeful in their movement and hand motions?
- Facial expressions—many speakers never look at themselves as they speak. I was once rejected as an applicant for a church worship job because the committee felt like I didn't smile enough. They were right.
- Vocal variety—Are speakers using all parts of their vocal range (high and low) and dynamics (loud and soft)? How about cadence? Are they speeding up and slowing down their rate of speech or just talking at the same speed?

- Content organization—Outside of inserting stories, many speakers don't follow the rule of 7. If the average attention span is 7 to 8 minutes, this rule says you should change something about your presentation every 7 minutes. Tell a story. Change the presentation medium. Include a video. Move around. Get the audience to participate verbally and/or physically.

- Practice, practice, practice—The more frequently a speaker gives a talk, the more they should practice and refine it before their first public speech. Michael Port gets his students to give their presentation to several live friendly audiences before the first public instance. Getting a coach or at least a knowledgeable friend to watch is smart. Michael Stelzner practices his keynote at least a dozen times. I always practice any talk at least five times before I give it. I want to be comfortable enough that I'm not overly reliant upon my slides.

  - **Please avoid the mistake I'm about to share with you.** When I was an intern, I was asked to read something during a church service. I practiced it the recommended five times. I read it flawlessly only to find that I had read the wrong selection. The audience was lost, and I was embarrassed!

  - Michael Port affirms another truth. "Practice makes permanent." The way you practice is super important. In his book, *Steal the Show*, Michael describes various ways to practice your talk. The most basic idea is to start with the most difficult part and rehearse that until you're confident. Then move to the next-most-difficult section. Move backward until you have the whole talk down.

  - Another true confession. During my college speech class, we were required to give a persuasive speech. I practiced mine but never felt totally confident with my conclusion. When it came time to give the speech, I froze when I got to the conclusion. I tried to back up and do it again, but my brain went blank. I quickly wrapped it up and ran for my seat. I silently vowed that I would never speak in public again. It took me three years before I tried again, but I wish I had known that it was my imperfect practice that led to my failure and not some inability to speak.

🍰 Understanding the audience—As we described with our mystery speaker above, speakers often fail when they try to give the same talk at every event they attend. Adaptation is essential. Jon Acuff, a very popular keynote speaker, always tries to get as much inside intelligence as he can before talks. He loves it when he gets to meet leaders in advance because he customizes it even more in light of the stories he hears.

Depending on the level of control you desire for the content, you may want to review every talk and even ask people to do dry runs for you (even if by video). The more you rehearse and prepare, the greater the number of things you can do to reinforce the experience. Just remember, if your speakers are speaking for free, you must be careful how much you demand of them, or they may speak negatively about you and/or not return.

Three journeys

Pulling all these different facets of your content together requires us to acknowledge that there are three different journeys that compose a great event. The content journey describes the intellectual and skill-oriented path someone needs to ascend to acquire the new knowledge, paradigm, or skills they came for. The emotional journey acknowledges the hero's journey that an attendee pursues to reach their goal. Finally, the delivery journey is the part that speakers, sponsors, and organizers embark on to deliver the experience. This includes emcees, production, staff, and volunteers.

When these three journeys form a perfect rope of experience, like a braided bread loaf, your guests will leave feeling confident that they have a new community, a new perspective, and renewed sense of purpose. When we fail one of these journeys, the attendee might still have a good experience, but it probably won't be great. If only one of these journeys is successful, you'll likely get lots of complaints. Even worse, you won't see the transformation you desire.

This chapter has explored the first and last journey. Chapter 11 will explore the emotional journey. Bringing them all together is the purpose of this book, but remember it's much more art than science. Yes, you can make a loaf with a machine (e.g., with a recipe), but handmade loaves are more lasting and beautiful. The same is true for your event.

Bread Bite

Question: How do you intentionally help your speakers create content that is customized for your audience?

Exercise:

1. Choose one of the following areas to explore:
   - Understanding your customer avatar
   - Knowing your customers' interests and needs
   - Defining your content style
   - Describe your ideal speaker experience (how do you make their day?)
2. Spend 10–15 minutes taking a first pass at how you would approach this.
3. Discuss your thoughts with your team and all the key stakeholders. What would they improve or change? What got them confused?
4. Decide now how you will implement these ideas into your event. When do you need to start? Who's in charge?

Chapter 8:

CONNECTIONS THAT MAKE THE DIFFERENCE

I'll never forget visiting Scotland in the summer of 1988. I participated in a choir tour across western Europe and the UK. Toward the end of the tour, we visited a remote part of Scotland. On the way to one village, our car got a flat tire. We stayed behind to repair the tire but got separated from the tour bus. No problem; we'll just ask for directions. Actually, it was a problem.

First, you need to know we were traveling with Dr. Edwin Hollatz, a communications professor. Imagine someone with a very rich rhetorician-style voice and a deep laugh. He infamously taught us to use our full vocal range by saying, "How now brown cow." Got a picture in your mind?

Now back to the story. The shepherd we stopped understood us perfectly, but he answered back in a dialect we couldn't understand. Between his thick accent and Dr. Hollatz' attempt to communicate on our behalf, we were no better off. We felt foolish for not being able to understand. After three attempts, we didn't want to keep asking, so we acted as if we understood. We went in the direction he pointed until we found a schoolboy who answered in Her Majesty's English and eventually found our destination.

I remember the feeling of being utterly helpless. I thought the guy was speaking English, but I recently retold this story and learned that the man was speaking Scots—a completely different language. Here I've been telling this story for decades with the wrong understanding of what happened. The new facts don't change the awkwardness I felt.

That's how it is with events. You'll have very clear memories of how certain things made you feel and who you were with. You may not remember all the facts correctly, but the people involved and the emotions create permanent markers in your brain.

In this chapter, I want to explore why relationships matter so much to your event. We've talked about the crew and the speakers, but it's time to focus on building connections with attendees.

Connections, a Top Goal

When people spend money to attend an in-person event, they are typically coming to learn and make important connections. Those connections could be for new business prospects, new hires, or new jobs. They may also seek a business expert, mentor, or a new circle of friends. Some come to deepen relationships with existing friends they only see once or twice a year. Still others come because they learn best in the context of a supportive community.

At this point, it's important for you to know your customers' desires and how to serve them. The best way is to ask. We will typically run a survey two months prior to the event to understand the learning and networking goals of our audience. Depending on your sales cycle, you might ask this immediately after they purchase the ticket, but if the event is more than three months away, they probably don't have meaningful answers to some of these questions. It's better to wait until you're within 60 days of the event—that's when people start making plans.

Note: We've found we'll get the highest response rate immediately after purchase, but you'll get more meaningful responses as you get closer.

What You Want to Know

Surveys will only reveal so much, as not everyone thinks about networking the way you need to understand it. My recommendation is to get on a call with at least five to ten customers and also get to know some of your super-connectors. Be sure to seek out some introverts or socially shy individuals for their perspectives. Lastly, talk to some of your international attendees if that's a significant part of your audience. Europeans approach networking very differently from Americans, for instance.

Here are three sets of questions to help define what your networking should look like.

What is your networking style?

Of course, most people wouldn't know how to answer that question so break it down for them with some of these questions:

- Are you gregarious or reserved?
- Where are you from?
- Do you prefer to have one or two deep conversations, or to meet a lot of interesting people at a networking event?
- Are you more likely to be the "life of the party" or to become someone's "new best friend?"
- How many new friends do you need to make for an event to feel fulfilling?

The aggregate of these answers will inform some of the other choices you make about the types of networking events you create.

Where do you prefer to network?

Some people will network from the moment they hit the ground, while others need a defined place and time. For some, a networking party should be quiet. Others like it loud with lots of alcohol. Some of your attendees prefer if you give them some structure with games or activities like speed networking. Others just want time on the schedule where they know they have time to meet people.

Note: if you can get your audience networking prior to the event, they will show up with a few friends. Megan Galloway at Campfire does a beautiful job of creating Zoom meetups where people make 10–12 new friends in the course of 45 minutes, all while having meaningful helpful conversations.

Create places within your venue where it's easy to sit down and have a conversation. This could be in the hallways, outside, or in your expo area. And don't overlook the places where people spend the most time: your session rooms. I've been to so many events where people get to a room early and immediately start to diligently study their phones. What if your emcees start the session five to ten minutes early and get the audience engaged with each other?

What are your networking goals?

As we hinted earlier, people have different objectives when they are networking. Some people come for great conversations or to have fun, while others come with very specific business goals. The design of your event should account for this.

Here are some questions to help define the relative importance of these objectives:

How important on a scale of 1 to 5 are the following objectives (1 being unimportant and 5 being highly important):

- 🍞 Lead gathering
- 🍞 Making new friends
- 🍞 Finding expert help
- 🍞 Discovering a new job
- 🍞 Recruiting job prospects
- 🍞 Having conversations about specific topics
- 🍞 Discovering peers who share my interests, industry, or job type

Putting it together

I attended an event pre-COVID where the agenda was nonstop sessions from 8 a.m. to noon then we took an hour lunch break and then it was more nonstop sessions from 1:30 to 6 p.m. The content was good, and there were so many amazing people in the room I would have loved to have met, but the agenda didn't allow for networking. It assumed people only came for the content. It's possible the event organizers knew their audience was just there to learn and didn't care to meet anyone else in the room, but I suspect they missed something that was important to their audience. Most of the sessions could have been enjoyed online.

That's an extreme example. Here's another:

I attended another event where they left 30 minutes to transition between sessions because of the massive building size and the time needed to scan badges. This could have been magical networking time, but the lines were mostly full of people who were busy on their phones. I observed very little purposeful networking taking place at a moment when everyone was forced into a pattern of behavior based on event logistics. It felt like we were being herded without providing encouragement to discover the amazing people who might be standing right around us.

Action: How might you do this differently for your event?

I've also seen events that add the word *networking* to a party and just assume that networking will happen. For a small percent of your audience, that's the only excuse they need. Your extroverted connectors don't need much permission to start talking to people. But I would venture that 50% or more of your audience will feel uncomfortable with this.

If your audience members told you they prefer quiet networking spaces, make sure you major in this. A loud dance band will make it hard for people to talk with each other. But if what they really desire is to let their hair down to open the door to conversations, then let the good times roll!

If you see that people really want to meet their industry peers, find ways that work. We call it "Table Talks." Others call it "Birds of a Feather" or "Round Tables." The goal is to create ways for people to gather around common topics, interests, or industries.

I was on a call recently where two friends told me they never would have met if we had not included a table for faith-based marketers. I know educators who organized dinners for higher education professors and found that more than 40 people attended. Another super-connector saw that we had over 50 attendees from Australia, so they created a Down Under meetup. It took someone studying the audience and finding ways to make these types of meetups possible.

5 ways to promote networking

There are many ways to promote networking at your event. Here is just a handful:

1. **Use your mobile app.** You don't have to pay tens of thousands of dollars to create a mobile app. We've used Facebook groups to facilitate networking and found it very effective, but you need to know if your audience already uses the app. Many third-party apps feature networking functions.

2. **Start 30 to 60 days before the event.** The more you can encourage people to meet fellow attendees prior to attending, the higher the chance they will feel comfortable and confident when they arrive.

3. **Catalyze your super-connectors.** Malcolm Gladwell called out the connectors as one of the three agents to create a Tipping Point moment. Depending on your audience makeup, you likely have 5–20% of your audience who consider themselves connectors— people who love introducing people to each other. Find who these people are. Activate them.

4. **Networking games can help.** While some people find games to be silly and a waste of time, many people see this as a low-threat way to meet people. Whether it's networking bingo, giant Jenga, a cornhole contest, or activations, you can help the socially shy find a way to enter into conversations without the awkwardness of figuring out how to say hello.

5. **Words matter.** When your audience hears the word *networking*, how do they respond? If it makes them think of the pushy card-toting salesman, maybe you want to choose a word like *connecting*. Whatever word you use, seek to implement it strategically throughout your event agenda. We found that using "Networking break" and "Networking

Plaza" encourages people to use the specified time and space for those reasons. We implicitly gave them permission to network and set the expectation that this is valued.

6. **Bonus**: Hire a networking ambassador. In our first year, Ambassador Mike Bruny approached us about being our networking ambassador. We loved the idea and have had a team of ambassadors every year whose goal is to help make strategic introductions throughout the event.

Three networking pitfalls to avoid

1. **The clingers**—We've all seen them or maybe we've even been one. Sometimes the socially awkward person finds a friendly face who makes them feel welcome, and now that person is their new best friend. The best way to help the clinger is to help expand their circle so they have more than one best friend. Get your super-connectors equipped to look for signs of clinging. They can come to the rescue.

2. **One and done**—One of my networking pet peeves is the person who makes a snap judgment that I'm not for them and within ten seconds has moved on. It's not *that* they have made the decision; it's the dismissive *way* in which it is done. One of the best remedies is to provide reminders that every story is worth hearing. This can be modeled by the networking ambassadors, in email communication, and from the stage.

3. **The Green Room**—Speakers love to hang out with each other. Your event might be one of the few places they get to see each other. To accommodate that, create a special party (or two) just for speakers. Otherwise, I encourage you to avoid a Green Room where speakers hang out all day. A speaker-ready room is needed so speakers can prepare for their talk, but otherwise, we have found it's better to invite the speakers to hang out with the audience they came to serve. There are always exceptions when you have super high-profile speakers, but generally speaking, you've invited the speakers because they have something to offer your audience.

Social Media and Networking for Events

Social media provides a tremendous free tool for your community to start getting to know each other. I've talked to event organizers who work with C-suite members who don't want to make themselves available to large conferences via social media. You need to know your audience, but for many events, social media provides an organic way for people to meet.

Here are a few additional tips for how to leverage the power of social media for your event:

1. **Use an event hashtag.** Platforms like Twitter, Instagram, and TikTok appreciate the power of hashtags, and this makes it easy for you and your audience to find others talking about your event. On Twitter, I encourage people to add the hashtag to their name or description so that they will be found by others who are looking.

2. **Find out where your audience spends time online.** It would make very little sense for you to create a group on Facebook if your audience exclusively spends time on LinkedIn. Ask them where they are. You'll still have to work to get them to see what you post, but at least you know you're on the right platform.

3. **Recruit some social media connectors**. I've found that many event logistics people I've hired don't enjoy being on social media. Find some people in your community who love to connect with others via social media. Get their help in building the kind of community they would want to be a part of.

4. **Create an engagement strategy.** Social media marketers create a communication plan to keep people engaging with their content. This is critical for event communities. A combination of tips, engagement questions, live video (or audio) sessions, and even Zoom-style events can create a great opportunity for people to meet.

5. **Provide ways to connect with your speakers.** Most of your speakers would love to connect with your audience. Consider creating a Twitter list of the speakers or a page where you share links to their accounts.

6. **Hold your pre-event orientation on social media.** I've found it super valuable to host a new attendee orientation using a streaming tool (e.g., Streamyard, Wave, eCamm) in our Facebook group. This allows us to share great content, and for attendees to discover each other through the chat.

7. **Experiment boldly.** The only way to find out how your audience will resonate is to try things. You'll never get all of your audience into an online community. We call it a success if we can get 50% engaged in our pre-event community.

Bread Bite

Making significant connections can be one of the most memorable parts of your event. When retelling stories, people often remember who they did things with even more than what they did or learned.

Creating a culture where it's easy to meet people can be one of your significant success factors. If you follow even a couple of suggestions from this chapter, you can start moving your event from ordinary to extraordinary, making it unforgettable.

Question: Is it obvious at your event that you value networking? How would an outsider know?

Exercise: Schedule some phone calls with people who consider themselves super-connectors and with others who are introverted and socially shy. Get to know what motivates each group. Find out about their fears. Ask what you can do at an event to help the connectors lean into their strengths and make even more connections. See if they would be willing to help you.

Chapter 9:

EVENT CULTURE:
A LITTLE YEAST GOING A LONG WAY

I'll never forget this greeting at the Customer Service Revolution put on by the DiJulius Group in Cleveland, Ohio. "Welcome, Mr. Mershon. We've been expecting you. Carisa here will escort you to your reserved seat. I hope you don't mind, but we gave you a seat right up front so you can see everything that is going on. If you need anything at all, please don't hesitate to ask."

I decided to test them, so I asked for a lens cleaner. Check. Then I asked for a special kind of hot tea. They found something similar and had it to me in minutes. Check.

I was impressed by how attentive the staff was to my needs. They were constantly checking in on me, but it never seemed intrusive. I felt like a VIP, but as I watched, I realized they were making all seven hundred guests feel like VIPs.

How do they do that?

I began asking lots of questions and learned this important lesson:

**Event culture can be cultivated and influenced
through a number of small but strategic decisions and actions.**

In this chapter, I will share five areas that all event organizers should think through as they create events where people feel like they belong and want to bring their friends.

But first, another story. . .

While watching the musical *In the Heights* by Lin-Manuel Miranda, I discovered myself increasingly connected to the story. By the time the musical ended, I grieved the loss of Abuela, the matriarch. I cheered for Benny to share his love for Nina. I sympathized with Nina's fear of sharing her failure with her family after losing her scholarship to Stanford. I felt Usnavi's angst over wanting to take his lottery winnings and return to the Dominican Republic to escape the challenges of life in Washington Heights. But when he chose to stay and invest his winnings in the neighborhood, I wanted to stand, cheer, and dance with the cast (in fact, I almost did cheer out loud, which would have been very embarrassing!).

You may not have seen this award-winning musical, but in my synopsis, you can see numerous universally relatable stories. Each story draws you in, making you feel like you're a member of the community. I counted fourteen relatable stories that I still remembered the following morning. The cumulative effect of these stories helped me see myself in the story and find meaning beyond the entertainment.

Why do I share this? This isn't a review of a musical, after all!

This story illustrates the most important point about culture: **culture is about how people connect, and that connection is made and strengthened by our common stories.** And while we can't create the culture we desire, we can influence it.

David Cummings, cofounder of Pardot, said, **"Corporate culture is the only sustainable competitive advantage that is completely within the control of the business owner."** Likewise, I would add that event planners have a competitive advantage over other events within your industry based on the culture you create.

For the record, no two events will ever have the same culture. Even if two events come up with the same solutions to the following criteria (which is unlikely), the way those solutions are implemented by people will be unique.

The Business Case for Focusing on Event Culture

"Culture has a way of keeping the people that fit and spitting out those who don't."
—Edward Stein

You may find yourself wondering how you're going to convince your CEO or CFO that focusing on the culture of your event is going to make you money. Let me ask you some questions:

- Have you ever attended an event where you had a bad experience and decided there on the spot that you'd never go back? Even more, did you tell your friends they shouldn't attend that event? **How much did that cost the event?**
- Have you ever had an event experience where something could have gone really poorly, but the event staff turned that experience into a favorite memory that you gladly tell others about? How many times have you told that story? What's the ROI on that experience?

I've had both of these experiences. My reactions led to a real bottom-line impact for those events. If many guests had a similar experience to mine, the cumulative impact would be very financially significant.

Still not convinced?

I'll never forget attending event A[11]. When I arrived, the lines were long, the lobby was confusing, and the people working the check-in desk seemed overwhelmed. When it was finally my turn, they treated me like I was the problem. Once I checked in, I had no idea where to go or what to do. No one made themselves available to answer questions. When I asked a convention center employee for directions, he pointed and acted like it was the easiest building in the world to navigate. I felt lost, abandoned, and frustrated. I decided I would never attend that event again and started telling my friends why they shouldn't go.

At event B, I also had a bad experience at check-in. The staff clearly didn't want to be there, but I soon ran into the event director, who gave me a private tour, introduced me to some leaders, and made sure I had a drink in my hand before I left the lobby. I still brag about that event.

The question for your CEO is: what's the value of free positive PR at our event? Or, what's the cost of negative PR from our event? Culture drives the experience your audience will have. It can create a context where people ignore little problems and focus on opportunities.

Five Strategies for Creating a Culture Your Community Will Love

A culture emerges whenever two or more people form ongoing relationships where they do things together. We don't usually call it culture until the group becomes larger than ten or more people, but the dynamics exist in all sizes of communities. For example, I know missionary kids who grew up in Papua New Guinea who created their own private language that they used just among siblings. Likewise, within a company, you'll find that different divisions and departments have their own unique subculture in terms of how they work and relate.

Edgar Schein, professor emeritus from Sloan School of Management at MIT, defines culture as

> **"A pattern of shared basic assumptions learned by a group
> as it solved its problems of external adaptation and internal integration. . .
> A product of joint learning."**
> —Edgar Schein

Another definition of culture comes from Delisc Simmons, Chief Culture Officer and Founder at The Culture Think Tank:

> "Culture is a collection of the behaviors of the people
> in a team, group or organization."
> —Delise Simmons

If culture is formed by people and how they behave together, there are three groups that have the most impact on an event:

1. Starting with your crew

Have you noticed the difference between the staff at Chick-fil-A and the staff at other fast-food restaurants? It's not their age. Almost all of these servers are teenagers or college students. The difference is in how friendly they are. Sometimes it becomes humorous to see how many times you can get them to say, "My pleasure."

A lead trainer at Chick-fil-A confided to me that they have very specific training guidelines for all new employees. While they do screen out those with an unfriendly disposition, all other skills are trained very intentionally.

We can do the same for our events. So, how do we do that?

Focus on your leaders. Everybody watches what the leaders say and do. If leaders reward certain behavior, you'll see more of that. If leaders ignore or tolerate certain behaviors, you'll also see more of that. If leaders discipline other kinds of behavior, those stories become legendary. If a leader doesn't practice the values you profess, you'll find everyone else ignoring them too.

That's why a leader's first job is to *define* the values. Their second job is to *demonstrate* them consistently. Their final job is to *defend* them.

I recently walked into my neighborhood Starbucks and met the new manager. I quickly sensed the culture of the team felt more focused, present, and friendly. The previous manager oversaw three stores. She couldn't give her focus to this one store, and the staff culture devolved a little bit.

I asked her why I experience such a diversity of experience in the Starbucks stores I've visited across the country. I estimate I've frequented at least fifty stores and maybe even a hundred. Some feel like the bar on Cheers, where everybody loudly cheers when you arrive, or like a big happy Italian family chatting everyone up and making them smile. Others feel very ordinary and forgettable.

She told me something profound: "Leaders set the culture. People follow leaders, not policies."

Train your leaders. Jeryn worked as an ER nurse before managing a Starbucks. She lamented that many health care facilities lose their customer-centric focus. Medicine is all about helping people heal, but when the staff starts to see patients as an annoyance to doing their job, the culture devolves into an antagonistic relationship. It seems to me that patients who don't trust their medical providers to be *for* them will start to complain, demand, and become irritable. If instead, they were treated with dignity, respect, and compassion, the same patient would become trusting and actively participate in their recovery.

Don't you think the latter scenario will be more likely to promote health and recovery?

Translate this to your event. Do your public-facing staff see your attendees and speakers as people deserving of their best service? Or do they get irritated because attendees prevent them from doing their job? What's most important to your leaders based on the actions of your staff?

You could ask the same question internally. We've recruited as many as 100 volunteers to produce our event each year. These people are often highly skilled, and many run their own businesses. They are accustomed to efficiency and personalization. If we treat them as pawns who just need to do their jobs, they will respond by giving minimal effort or maybe even vacating their shifts. If instead, we show appreciation and esteem, we will get above-and-beyond service. Our event will become better.

Serena has volunteered for at least four years at our events. She lives in Australia and could not travel in 2022. She lamented for months that she wouldn't be able to come. We knew she has incredible customer service skills, so we invited her into our online community management team. While there, she realized we have an opportunity to make our live-streaming product amazing. She wants to get as much value out of the event as possible for herself. As a result, she offered to lead our livestream moderation team. She wants to make sure it's amazing for her and will work to ensure the same for all other attendees.

That loyalty didn't happen overnight. I would never ask or expect a first-year volunteer to do something so lavish. But after years of partnership and mutual encouragement, she can't imagine not being part of our event.

Keep it simple and memorable. I've been impressed by the caliber of people who volunteer at our events. Some are millionaire philanthropists who enjoy helping others. Some are executive nonprofit leaders who just don't have budgets. One of our longest-tenured volunteers is a Hall of Fame speaker with the National Speakers Association (NSA) and he loves volunteering at our events because very few people know who he is.

But no matter how smart or skilled these people are they don't know your event the way you do. In fact, they probably haven't thought about your event until they show up so it's critical to keep it simple. If you want them to impact the culture, focus on the behaviors that will most dramatically impact the culture.

We found that the "Never/Always" exercise from the The DiJulius Group is a powerful tool for deciding what behaviors you want to avoid and what behaviors you want to accentuate. The following chart demonstrates the ten pairs of behaviors they focus upon. You might find you want to replace some of these or adapt them to language that makes sense internally, but it's easy for anyone to grasp what you value.

Never	Always
Point	Show them the way
Say "No"	Find a way to say "yes"
Say "I don't know"	Find out the answer
Show frustration publicly	Be a duck
Pass by a problem	Stop, engage, and help solve the problem
Make excuses	Own it, even if it's not your fault
Gossip or complain	Remember you're always on stage
Deliver bad news via email	Make it right
Leave things to chance	Be prepared
Cold transfer	Warm transfer

Credit: Inspired by working with The Dijulius Group

Look out for unintended consequences. People watch what you do far more than they listen to what you say. For example, if you train your team to "Greet everyone with a friendly smile" but never smile yourself and always avoid difficult customers, you send a message to your team that you don't really mean it.

One year, I developed a simple scheme for teaching our staff to greet and serve attendees. It utilized the hand as a mnemonic device. The message is simple: Welcome people warmly. Take them where they want to go. Always invite people into deeper conversation. Find out what's most important to them, and then seek to link them with other attendees.

It was quite easy to understand, but it turns out I'm better at developing mnemonic devices than I am at smiling. During the conference, our accountant came up to me, held up his hand in a smile formation, and said, "Smile, Phil!"

I was caught. I can make excuses for why it's hard for me to smile, but it doesn't matter. I can smile with my eyes even if my mouth doesn't form a perfect smile. But I had become distracted by my work and didn't model the joy I asked of others.

Consequence can be subtle. What message does it send if your leader disappears for extended periods of time?

True story. In the early years of our event, I held the firm belief and practice of daily naps (I still believe in them, but I practice them differently.) There's a ton of research on the benefits of naps[12]. And frankly, when I'm running our event, I typically only sleep 3–4 hours at night. A nap becomes necessary. But after one conference, I realized I couldn't keep taking naps during our conference, even if they were only for 20 minutes.

Here's what unintentionally happened.

I encouraged everyone to take care of themselves, and if that required a nap, to do it. On the busiest day of our event, I made sure to grab 20 minutes of downtime, and it included a nap in our first few years. In fact, my naps became such a part of the event that the team pulled together a sleeping bag and pillow to put in storage and labeled it "Phil's sleeping bag." That felt embarrassing to see. I was the only person taking a nap during the day.

But we had a contractor who took it too far. They disappeared during the middle of the day for a couple of hours. When confronted about it, they admitted going back to their hotel room to take a nap. Being gone for 2 hours was unacceptable, but I couldn't fully blame them. They didn't know that I limited my nap to 20 minutes and that I never left the property. Instead, they thought, "Well, if Phil can take a nap, so can I. Besides, he told me to take care of myself."

I bred a culture where people saw me as tired and unavailable. It also gave permission to staff to do as they desired. My core team knew that I worked very hard, but others saw me as distant and weak.

What's funny is I preach the right things to our team about the things we value. We want people who go the extra mile. We desire service, excellence, and awareness.

I worked very hard, but I didn't see how this one small action affected the culture.

Today we have gotten rid of the bedding. It's okay for me to slip away for a few minutes to take a break, but I don't make a production out of it and I seek to model the behaviors I want from my staff and volunteers.

We all know it doesn't work to say, "Do what I say and not what I do." If our kids know better so will our staff. And the effect will be a growing sense of distrust in the culture, people who are in it for themselves, and palpable frustration.

Examine your cultural impact. There are two ways to assess your impact on culture.

First, look at the culture you desire to create. You've probably written down values and statements that express how you want your culture to function. Look at that. Get honest feedback on how well you and your leadership exhibit those values. Are there any obvious incongruencies? Which are the most detrimental if you don't fix them? Focus on those first.

Second, get people who know you well to answer this question: "Based on my behavior, what would you say are the most important things to me?" Ask a variety of people to answer this. Don't be afraid to ask your spouse and some close friends in addition to work colleagues, bosses, and customers.

As you look at these two lists, celebrate places where your values match up with the culture you seek. But also look at places where you can improve.

Hire or recruit the right staff. After your leaders, everything flows from your core team, so make sure they embody your core values. Let me illustrate why this is important, and I'll elaborate on how to choose your values below.

I once spoke for an event where I was well cared for until I arrived at the event. Once I checked in, I was ignored by the event staff. It was as if I didn't matter any longer. I had to figure out how to take care of my own audio/visual needs, and when I asked questions, it became clear I was bothering the staff members. It was a yucky experience and one I wouldn't want for my speakers.

It's possible the staff were having a bad day, but I think it was more an issue of training and having the right people on the job.

If your staff are more focused on efficiency and process than they are customer service, your customers will feel that. At every step of the way, challenge your team to think, *How will this affect the customer experience?*

Jesse Cole of the Savannah Bananas is a master at this. He calls it Fans First. That's the rubric through which they make every decision. When I attended my first game, I observed that some of the concession staff didn't seem to embody this value. I asked him about this and he became livid. He shared that due to a massive number of people calling in sick, he had to rely on temporary staff. They had not been trained in the Fans First philosophy. He shared that it was his top priority to fix that.

Speakers are the heartbeat of your event. Other than your staff, no one influences the culture of your event more than your speakers and sponsors.

Depending on the type of event you run, the speakers may have the greatest impact on culture.

Think about it. Your attendees come to learn from the experts and their peers. If speakers are unapproachable or leave the event as soon as they are done, that communicates that they are better than everyone else. If, however, speakers make themselves available to answer questions and help people throughout the event, this creates a learning culture.

There is certainly a place for high-profile speakers who require security teams and therefore make it impossible for that person to mingle with the throngs. I remember seeing Serena Williams speak at a conference. There's no way I would have been allowed close to her. I also remember Malcolm Gladwell made himself available to sign books and answer questions for an hour after his presentation. But as soon as he finished, he was ushered away. That's reasonable.

Rethink the green room. Speakers love the "green room" as a place to prepare themselves before they speak. That's valuable. But at many events, the green room becomes a place where speakers hide from the masses and just hang out with their friends.

> **What is a green room?** According to Wikipedia, in show business, the green room is the space in a theater or similar venue that functions as a waiting room and lounge for performers before, during, and after a performance or show when they are not engaged onstage.

If your event aims to create a community of approachability, consider getting rid of the traditional green room and instead create a ready room where speakers can prepare, but don't let it become a place to hang out.

Serve your speakers with excellence.

I love to ask speakers about their favorite drinks so we can surprise them with their favorite hot tea before they speak. For a couple of years, we would follow what they spoke about on social media and order them a unique gift tailored to their interests. That became challenging when we had over 100 speakers.

Speakers will love your event and serve your audience with excellence if you take great care of them. Become students of their interests. Make sure to have customer-focused staff who will handle all the details leading up to the event.

Most speakers love the opportunity to mingle with their peers. Consider hosting a speaker party that allows time for them to network and catch up.

Find creative ways to feature your speakers. Most speakers I know don't want to just come and speak one time and have nothing else to do. And while they certainly tend to create their own opportunities, most speakers love having options. Here are a few:

- ♟ **Organize speaker meetups**. Consider creating a dedicated time and place where speakers can have informal conversations or question/answer sessions.

- ♟ **Make Q&A easy**. Most people don't like to ask their questions of speakers on an open mic during a session (and I would argue that most of the questions asked in this context probably shouldn't have been asked, but I digress). Create an easy way for people to ask questions immediately following a session. It could be as simple as inviting the speaker to hang out for an hour in the hallway. Attendees and speakers all love this. In fact, we have speakers brag about how long they went and how many people stayed!

- ♟ **Facilitate round table discussions**. Ask your speakers to facilitate conversations around their expertise. Note: just be clear that this isn't another presentation opportunity or a sales meeting. We've had speakers do both of those things, and attendees get frustrated.

- ♟ **Advertise speaker-led gatherings**. If it makes sense, let attendees know about free gatherings being organized by speakers. Perhaps create a listing of these events as long as they are free and adjacent to your event.

2: Space jam: culture shaped by space

> "We will postpone a retreat until we get the right space."
> —Howard Cleveland, event planner

Space travel seems increasingly likely in our lifetime. Can you imagine planning the first learning event in outer space? While SpaceX already hired someone to plan events for customers going into outer space, I'm talking about a learning experience for the masses.

How would your event be different if it was held in outer space? That might be a very effective idea-generating question for you and your team to ponder. Here are a few fun questions to deepen the conversation:

- How do you communicate effectively when everyone is on headsets?
- What do you do if a comet interferes with your electronics?
- How do you lean into the visual backdrop of outer space without feeling cliché?
- Do you need to worry about seating configurations, or should you allow everyone to float around at will?
- How can you make the meals memorable when everything is dehydrated?
- While the whole trip will be unforgettable, how do you make it transformational and not just a great story?

These questions should spark your mind to consider some important ideas that will make your next terrestrial event more impactful. Speaking of earth, the way we use the physical space has a dramatic impact on the culture that emerges in our event. I've found many event professionals don't think these things through beyond the vibe and feel they want to create.

There are several considerations when it comes to physical space that affects the culture of your event—some of these you can control. Others you adapt to. **Proximity** or how close people are to one another has a dramatic psychological impact on learning, comfort, and a sense of safety. More on that below.

Space layout affects people subconsciously. A square seating arrangement feels more formal whereas adding curvature feels less formal and more inclusive. Seating people in small circles sends an immediate message that people will actively participate as opposed to passively watching and listening.

Some of the mundane choices you make about aesthetics can massively impact your culture. Choices about colors, lighting, scents, and furniture all add up to create a vibe that can either contribute to the culture you seek or work against it.

At Social Media Marketing World, we learned to make intentional choices that reflect the fun, vibrant, energetic, and connection-focused culture we seek. We started by adding tropical aromas to the air as people check in. It's subtle, but we want people to feel relaxed and refreshed after a long day of traveling. We use live plants wherever possible, as opposed to artificial plants, because we want the air to feel fresh and alive. We used vibrant beachy colors to keep the energy alive but keep enough elements that feel professional so people know that serious business can be conducted here.

One year, we convinced a hotel to brew large vats of coffee and place industrial fans near the doors to blow the aroma of coffee as people arrived for a networking function. We wanted people to linger over the coffee, have deeper conversations, and spend time talking with our sponsors and speakers. It's hard to know if it worked, but there's a reason Starbucks blows coffee aromas throughout their stores.

A whole chapter could be written just about selecting the right building that supports the business goals you have and the culture you seek, but sometimes the location is more important than having the right building. As long as the building has the potential to be changed, you can create amazing experiences most anywhere—experiences are ultimately about people doing things together that lead to extraordinary results.[13]

Understanding proxemics: an underappreciated aspect of events

Proxemics is the study of how people use space and the effects it has on communication, behavior, and social interaction. Edward Hall, the founder of the study of proxemics, put it like this: "Proxemics is the interrelated observations and theories of humans' use of space as a specialized elaboration of culture."[3]

Hall looks at four different ways people engage that relate directly to how people gather and learn at conferences.

- **Intimate**: This is for close conversations with 1–3 other people.
- **Personal**: This is for close friends and family, typically no more than 10 or 12 people.
- **Social distance**: For gatherings of 10–40 people, primarily acquaintances.
- **Public**: Gatherings of 40 to infinity. You could break this into small, medium, large, and mega gatherings.

Depending on the cultural background of your audience (e.g., Latino, African, Asian, Canadian), the personal space needed between people might be more or less.

If you force people to sit very close to one another and this makes them uncomfortable, they are unlikely to stick around to talk with each other. Conversely, if you force people to sit too far apart you might find people prefer to stay by themselves.

Having the barrier of a table or coffee table can often help people feel more comfortable with each other.

One aspect of proxemics is that many people learn best in smaller conversations, which is why so many events try to get people to have conversations with one or two people in huddles. This can feel very forced, but if conducted strategically with the right questions, it can lead to the best learning as people have meaningful conversations.

Questions to ask yourself:

- Who is my primary audience?
- Do they tend to be extroverted or introverted?
- Do they enjoy large groups or small-group interactions?
- Are they gregarious or more withdrawn?
- When I look at pictures of these people do they tend to stand close to each other or farther apart?

I lead a conference for social media marketers. While marketers come in many different colors and forms, I believed that they would be outgoing and love to interact with each other. I was surprised to find many social media marketers are introverts and felt just fine working on their phones as opposed to approaching strangers.

Table Talks

We decided a way to help people meet each other was by creating smaller places where they could meet people with similar interests. We called these Table Talks (others call it round tables or "birds of a feather") where 5–8 people gather to discuss a topic. Someone takes the role of facilitator to make sure everyone gets a chance to talk.

Dunbar's rule of 140

Social scientist Robin Dunbar theorized that most people can only maintain relationships with somewhere between 100 and 250 people, with the average being 148. That means within a large event of thousands of people, we need to make it possible for attendees to feel comfortable with smaller groups. Likewise, our staff can't possibly maintain relationships with thousands of people, but we can with groups of 100–200.

When the group becomes larger, people tend to pull away and blend in.

How might you break your event into smaller groups that create the safety and comfort that your attendees crave?

3: Stories

Whether at a family gathering, a class reunion, or a large cultural event, communities find their identity through the stories they remember. Families laugh about Uncle Jerry and the time he drank from the fish bowl. Grown men become like boys when they remember the stories and pranks from their college days. Dead Heads rehearse all the famous concerts they've attended. Nations remember their leaders, wars, and independence days.

In these ways, stories shape the history and language we use. But stories also have a way of predicting and defining behavior.

When I worked for Koch Industries, the stories were legendary of the executives who worked 60- and 70-hour weeks so they could be seen by the CEO when he left for the day. That inspired other younger executives to also work long hours. Then there were the stories of people who got fired with no questions asked when they were caught looking at porn on company time and computers. Conversely, stories zoomed around the company about the trader who lost a million dollars on a trade that went bad and instead of being fired, he was kept around because the leaders didn't want to waste that expensive lesson.

If you look at those three examples, you can quickly discern a cultural pattern that employees seek to live within. Hard work is respected; the longer, the better. Don't cross certain moral lines. Don't be afraid to take risks as long as you keep learning.

The same thing happens at events. If you watch social media after your event, you'll quickly notice the stories that your speakers and attendees remember. You have the chance to influence the culture through the stories you celebrate and rehearse.

Expect Serendipity

At our conference, Heather sent me this note telling me how she found future clients at our conference just by being open to serendipitous conversations. I love telling these stories to people at our conference. It invites openness to the unexpected. As a result, I believe people are far more willing to initiate conversations with anyone and everyone. That has a profound impact on the event's culture.

"Dear Phil, thank you for inviting me to volunteer at SMMW16. I took a chance, and it changed the course of my career. You may remember I served on the networking team. I helped many people make meaningful connections, but I never imagined I might be the answer to someone's request. Well, one day, a distinguished cowboy came up to the table and asked me if I knew of a social media marketing manager to join their remote team. He told me about the company and guaranteed that whoever took on the role would never be the same. Well, he was right. I told him I knew exactly who he should interview, and by the end of the week, I had signed the contract. That September, they flew the entire team to Jackson Hole, Wyoming. It was four days of team training, professional development, horseback riding, and fine dining. It was magical and never could have happened if I hadn't been to SMMW and been open to a serendipitous moment. Here's my encouragement to everyone going to a conference: 'Show up, say yes, and expect serendipity.'"

—Heather Myklegard

Sometimes, you need to manage the stories being told.

In 2019, Mark Schaefer, our closing keynote speaker, wanted to end on a high note. We created a spectacular indoor fireworks show that had people taking confetti selfies. The unexpected consequence was the confetti guns triggered some people with PTSD. Some thought it sounded like gunshots were going off, and we hadn't provided any warning. Fortunately, those who were triggered didn't speak up too loudly, but we definitely learned a lesson to be aware of everyone in your audience.

Then there's the story of a homeless man who was taking a bath in the women's bathroom. It was traumatic at the time, but now it's legendary. It also causes our staff to be diligent in watching out for each other.

I joined the hospitality team for a while at Life Church. They utilize storytelling very well to reinforce what's important to them. For example, the leader shared a story of someone we'll call "Nick." Nick made fun of his sister for attending church. She knew that he is a huge Harry Potter fan, so when our campus decided to decorate the lobby with a Harry Potter theme, she told him about it. He wondered how that fits in at church. She told him he would need to see for himself. He came expecting to ridicule the church. He left saying that it was "Weird, but in a good way." That became the theme for the day: "Be weird—but in a good way." It was a small story that reminded people of why they are doing what they are doing.

Great leaders find ways to frequently tell stories that reinforce the culture.

> **Recommendation:** Become very good at capturing and telling the stories that reinforce what you want your event to be about.

4: Activities

Cultural anthropologists study the behaviors and rituals of people to understand the culture. As event anthropologists, we seek to understand and influence the culture through the strategic insertion of activities and rituals that create a culture conducive to the community we seek to build.

It's not just which activities we choose, but also how we do them. Most events have networking parties or events, but I'll bet you've attended some that feel like a middle school dance where the boys and girls all stand against the wall refusing to take the first step. Why do some parties feel inviting and others feel forced?

Some events I've attended assume that if you open the doors to a cool venue, offer food and drinks, and call it a networking party, people will love it. Unfortunately, that's like opening a garage door, walking inside, and calling yourself a car. A person can never become a car, but a party can actually become a community-building event when people feel welcome and safe and have easy ways to engage.

Focus on powerful moments. When people remember your event, they likely won't remember every point from any given session. They will remember the people they met, how they felt, and the context where they learned something valuable.

Unfortunately, many events undermine those moments by focusing on logistics instead of transformation. I remember attending a conference where a very helpful and powerful keynote took place. However, as soon as the speaker finished and we were dismissed, loud music began to play to encourage us to leave the room for our next session. I couldn't even hear myself think. In less than a minute, I had forgotten some of the key lessons I wanted to remember from that session. I found myself frustrated by the organizers' desire to move us out of the room instead of giving us time to reflect on what we learned.

What are the most powerful moments at your event? Chapter 11 dives deeply into the customer journey, so for the sake of understanding how the schedule impacts culture, let's focus on common moments that shape culture:

- 🎂 **Welcome experience**—When people arrive, what does it look and feel like? Are they greeted warmly, or is it more of an efficient experience? What about the experience after they check in?
- 🎂 **Timeliness**—Do you start and end sessions on time, or do you treat the schedule as more of a guide? Does a schedule even exist?
- 🎂 **Proximity**—How close do you seat your guests to each other? Are they seated in rows or circles?
- 🎂 **Sound**—Do you play music during the event? If so, what kind? How loud is it? Are you intentional about how you're using music to set the tone?

- ♨ **Color and smell**—What colors are you using? Are there specific smells associated with your event?
- ♨ **Peak moments**—What are the collective experiences that you think people will remember? How can you intensify those moments? What are things you can do when everyone is together that they will talk about later?

5: Values

Values create a community of people who serve each other. I recently visited a doctor's office for the first time. You would have thought I was a bank robber based on how the front desk staff treated me. They were suspicious and seemed annoyed that I would ask them a question. When I called back later to get the X-rays, they told me that I wasn't allowed to have **my** X-rays. I finally spoke with a manager who was a bit apologetic.

Compare that to my primary care physician or my physical therapist's office, where everyone understands the power of service. Every staff person wears a smile and is happy to serve in any way they can. No one wants to visit the doctor, but it doesn't need to be painful.

Conversely, most people choose to attend your event because of its promised benefits. But if your staff seems distracted or unhappy to be there, it will negatively affect the experience. What if instead you train people to anticipate needs and provide "white glove" service? If you do this, people will give you the benefit of the doubt if something goes strong.

When someone comes to your team with a complaint, look at that as an opportunity to make that person's day. You may not be able to fix their immediate problem (for example, the session they wanted is full), but you can give them insights into other ways to learn that material or connect with the speaker. You could offer them a small gift (we hand out coffee gift cards) as an apology.

This happens frequently: A few years ago, Lucy lost her luggage on the way to our conference. We've instructed our team to find ways to solve problems, and we've even given some team members the authority to spend up to a certain amount without getting approval. In the case of Lucy, the team found her an event T-shirt and paid for a taxi to take her to buy some clothes and overnight sundries. She hardly missed any of the conference and was able to survive until her luggage arrived the next day.

Most service opportunities are very small. Someone gets lost. The temperature is too hot or too cold. Rooms are full. A person feels overwhelmed. When team members become good listeners, they can turn challenges into highlight moments.

Remember in Chapter 1 how a toothbrush resulted in a profitable memory? Your event can produce those moments, too.

Define the values you care about. When you spend time understanding your values, it helps identify the right team members. It also shapes what activities you focus on and how you do them.

The following are values I care about when recruiting team members. Your list might be similar or different, but notice how these will inevitably shape our culture:

- 🎂 **Service mindset**—We need people who place the needs of others before their own. This includes the ability to anticipate needs, observe opportunities, and a willingness to respond even when you don't have all the answers. I envision the white-gloved staff of a 5-star restaurant serving my attendees, but with the vibe of a Southern California lifeguard.
- 🎂 **Attention to detail**—Events are complex systems of thousands of details. While we need friendly, happy people, we also need people who love checklists and processes.
- 🎂 **Flexibility**—Running events is the fifth most stressful job on the planet. One of the best strategies for dealing with stress is remaining flexible. We like to say, "Never let your frustration show publicly. Always let it roll off your back like a duck." The best event coordinators do this with grace and ease. I've had staff who became overwhelmed by the thousands of decisions that need to be made. They let their stress be seen by the team. As a result, everyone felt stressed. Speakers even said about one staff member, "She scares me. I don't want to work with her." Not a good signal.

- 🏅 **Emotional Intelligence**—People who are self-aware tend to have a better awareness of those around them. I wrote an article on LinkedIn called "Showing Up Powerfully.[14]" Read it for more insights into this.
- 🏅 **Integrity**—Do they do what they say? Are they the same person in private as they are in public? Ask around. You'll be surprised sometimes.
- 🏅 **Event experience**—Do they have a track record of volunteering and running events, or do they just like the idea of working on your event because of the free ticket or the celebrity speakers you're bringing?
- 🏅 **Inquisitive**—Find people who are naturally curious.

> "Questions are taken for granted rather than given a starring role
> in the human drama. Yet all my teaching and consulting experience
> has taught me that what builds a relationship, what solves problems,
> what moves things forward is asking the right questions."
> – Edgar H. Schein, *Humble Inquiry: The Gentle Art of Asking Instead of Telling*

Defend your values. What do I do when someone's a bad role fit, but a good cultural fit? We had a staff member who was an excellent project manager. She worked extra hard, kept things super organized, and was ready to lead a team. Unfortunately, when she got to the event, she became red-faced and started stressing out her team. We quickly learned that she had not been well-prepared for the on-site job, and she was being asked to do things for which she wasn't a good job fit. We did the best we could to support her during that event, but then we worked to make sure she was better supported for the following year.

If you have a good cultural fit, work hard to figure out what's not working so they can perform the work they love and you need. If, however, you have someone who is not following your values, you need to be quick to defend the culture you have defined.

Edgar Schein says, "Culture is what you settle for." Said in a different way, culture is the result of the worst behaviors we're willing to tolerate.

Some of our high-performing team members solicited business while wearing staff shirts. We had to confront those people. In some cases, we did not invite them back because they didn't see the conflict of interest.

Bread Bite

Remember that in the long run, culture trumps performance.

Question: Do your customers talk about your event culture? If they do, what do they say?

Exercise: Take the Event Culture Survey (go to philmershon.com/unforgettable/culturesurvey) with all your key stakeholders and core team members. Compare your results. Come to an agreement on the most important elements of your culture you want to focus on.

Chapter 10:

CREATING CONDITIONS FOR CHANGE: EXPECTING SERENDIPITY

I'll never forget a conversation I had with Dana Malstaff, CEO & Founder of Boss Mom. Our goal was to talk about how emcees can create the conditions for meaningful connections inside an event. Instead of talking about it, we did it. We shared experiences and insights freely, discovering many ways our vision for events align. Here's the problem: We had only scheduled 30 minutes for our call.

After 28 minutes, I said, "Well, I guess I should share why I scheduled this call."

We both laughed and extended the call. We recognized the importance of the conversation and valued the distraction.

I could feel shame because I wasn't productive in accomplishing my mission. Instead, I found myself curious and affirmed that what I desire to create is possible and needed.

Imagine with me. Attendees at your next event walk away with a handful of meaningful action items that feel doable and significant. What if they also held the names of three to five new connections that feel like allies and friends?

What if it was just one or two powerful relationships and action steps? Would that still be worth it?

People will always take pictures of the parties, reunions, and highlight-reel moments, but they will remember how they felt when that new idea sparked or when they entered a meaningful conversation.

During our conference in 2018, I challenged my team to create a list of two or three things they wanted to see happen during the conference for it to take on a deeper level of personal meaning. I shared my list halfheartedly with a team member because my top goal at the event is to be a host that creates those moments for everyone else. I'm not there looking for personal benefit.

You can imagine my surprise when all three of my wishlist items happened before the first session ever started. All three of them took place in the hallway during brief conversations with friends. If I hadn't set the intention, I'm not sure I would have noticed.

Lasting change normally takes hard work, but the impetus for change often comes in an unexpected form. It might take a visit to the Emergency Room to get you to take your health seriously. A "chance" conversation with a friend might get you to finally start that new venture. An idea shared at a conference might introduce the liberating thought that helps you finally believe in your ability to change the world in a specific way.

Serendipity is at the heart of all kinds of change.

Sparking Serendipity on Purpose

"If content is king, conversation is queen. If you're thinking about the people you met, then you know what makes an event worth returning to is the incredible people it connects us with."
—Brudis Limarr III

How do you spark serendipity on purpose? You can't make it happen. You *can* create the right conditions and spark the flint.

If you're a Survivor fan, you probably enjoy watching the fire-lighting challenge. The ones who win always know how to create the conditions that allow a spark to turn into a flame and then into a robust fire.

Here are four basic elements for creating the conditions for serendipity:

Element #1: Space

Have you ever walked out of a conference and said, "I felt like I was drinking out of a firehose." As an event organizer or speaker, it's easy to read that as a compliment. We think they said, "There was so much good stuff, I couldn't possibly take it all in."

But what if your customers really mean, "I felt blasted by the information and opportunities and never found time to take a breath or find those deeper moments." That's a lot like a heavy wind blowing on a small spark—the flame will never catch.

> **"Slow down before you speed up."**
> —Mimika Cooney

It's easy to think you need to hit them hard and fast or you'll lose them. My recommendation is to treat this like a long-distance race. Distance runners will typically start out a bit faster in their first mile to get into a good position and then settle into their ideal pace. After that, it's only for key moments or the end of the race when they sprint.

We hope our attendees will spend time setting their intentions and goals before they arrive. The reality is, less than half will. We need to be intentional about creating the different kinds of spaces people need.

Here are three types of space to consider:

1. **Physical space**—Do you have places where people can sit alone or in quiet conversations? Do you have natural beauty or creative elements that might inspire bigger thoughts or conversations?
2. **Temporal space**—How have you designed your schedule? Do you schedule sessions one after another for four hours with no scheduled

breaks or opportunities for reflection or conversation? I've seen this happen. It becomes very uncomfortable. Create breaks that are long enough to have a conversation (or two) and take care of your biological needs (coffee, food, bathroom) and still get to whatever is next on the schedule.

3. **Emotional space**—People need to feel safe. Our human nature is to enter the fight, flight, or freeze mode when we encounter danger or the unknown. People won't seek serendipity if they are scared. One way to create psychological safety is through communicating and showing how you're taking care of personal safety (security guards, health protocols, and a well-organized event). People notice that you've thought of tiny details and that puts them at ease (see section on the ROI of a toothbrush). A second way is by helping people find their tribe quickly. We all want to feel like we belong and are known. At our events, we try to start this long before they arrive.

Element #2: Expectation

If you're not looking for serendipity, you will rarely find it. I constantly say, "Expect Serendipity." I know of countless stories of people finding jobs, partnerships, and valuable help because they were looking for opportunities.

Fiona came to our event as a speaker and a thought leader in the sports industry. After the event, she caught me at the wrap-up party and told me about the transformational conversation she had with a man named Peter. They started talking after a session and realized their businesses were in similar stages of growth. The conversation intensified. They both realized that was why they came to the conference, so they decided to skip the next two sessions.

Fiona told me she was looking for opportunities and immediately took action when one presented itself.

How do you create expectation? Share stories. Talk about possibilities. Encourage people to dream.

The adage goes, "People notice what they are looking for." If people describe for themselves what they seek, they will be far more likely to notice it.

Element #3: Curiosity

Some say, "Curiosity killed the cat." I say a lack of curiosity kills the soul.

Jon Berghoff, Founder and CEO at the XChange Approach, teaches the power of appreciative inquiry. He believes by asking the right questions, we can quickly tap the collective wisdom of a group or organization. This will lead to change at a much faster rate than an individual can effect.

One of the keys is to stay curious in every conversation and moment. It may sound lofty and unachievable, but start by staying present in the moment. When you are in a conversation, focus on that person and don't wonder about who else you could be talking with. Ask questions. Listen for the story behind the story.

Every person has a story worth sharing. Steve Preston, president of Goodwill, once worked on the Cabinet for President George W. Bush. He marveled at the way President Bush prepared for every meeting and meal. His staff would do research and give him things to read and review to prepare. He would read enough to have an interesting and informed conversation with each person he met. No matter who they were.

Of course, we can't do that at a conference for every person we meet. Or could we? But what if you retain that level of curiosity about the experience and expertise of each person you meet? How will that make the other person feel? What if instead of entering a debate, you sought to understand how someone reached the conclusions and opinions they hold?

No person corners the market on truth or wisdom. In fact, information creation has grown exponentially in recent decades. Just since 2010, the amount of information stored online has grown by 5,000%. Information is a commodity and easily discovered. Meaningful relationships are gold that deserves deliberate mining. If you keep digging, you might even find diamonds or mithril (the fictitious, but extremely precious metal found in *The Lord of the Rings*).

Element #4: Lingering

I love watching cowboys herding cattle, or border collies herding sheep. But I hate being treated like a cow or sheep at events. Have you experienced that?

As soon as a session is over, the audio/visual technician cranks up the music loud enough that you have no choice but to leave the room.

I'll never forget this happening at a large conference. A keynote session just ended and the content was particularly stimulating. I couldn't wait to discuss one of the points with my peers. But as soon as the emcee closed the session, the music cranked up to 10. I couldn't think or hear my peers. We all stood up and quietly waited in line to escape the noise.

By the time I reached the lobby, I could no longer remember what I wanted to discuss. Instead, we turned to our basic needs of food, coffee, and bathrooms—the moment was lost.

If you want people to have meaningful conversations, you need to create space for it. Here are a few ways to do that:

- **Bake it into the agenda.** Instead of having short breaks that barely leave enough time to grab some coffee and visit the bathroom, make some of your breaks long enough that people feel comfortable lingering for a few moments after each session.
- **Invite attendees to linger.** Invite your emcees to create short moments before and after sessions where they ask stimulating questions that can lead to deeper conversations. Sometimes lingering is a bad thing: we don't want bad odors to linger around. But when it comes to the pursuit of meaningful conversation, those who stick around are way more likely to find it than those who quickly move on.
- **Design options.** Some people may prefer to do this in silence whereas others want to process it out loud. Some may desire to ask follow-up questions of the presenter and others may want to be guided through a reflective process. Provide some options.
- **Create a networking track**. What if in addition to your content tracks you had a simultaneous track just for networking? It might include fireside chats with speakers, round table conversations, and space for 1:1 appointments that could be scheduled through an app or on-site.

Bonus: Engineering

Artificial intelligence (AI) and smart technology can be one of your best allies in the pursuit of serendipity. Braindate believes it's possible to engineer serendipity. In fact their tagline is:

> **"A human-centric, crowdsourced platform that empowers attendees to connect over topic-driven conversations."**
> —Braindate.com

Mobile apps and social media sites make it easier for people to find the people they want to meet and connect with. For these tools to work best, however, you need a team of people working as concierges. Otherwise, you're still leaving things largely to chance.

Bread Bite

You can't force serendipity, but you can create the conditions for powerful connections and memories to be formed. Just a few intentional choices on your part could very well spark some life-changing moments.

Question: How will you plan for serendipity at your events? Using this chapter as a guide, identify 2–3 intentional decisions you can make for your next event.

Exercise: Think about a time when you had a serendipitous encounter recently. Write down the story and get as specific as you can about the details. Look back and see how many things had to align to facilitate that moment. What can you learn about how you can create the conditions for those kinds of moments?

Chapter 11:

CRAFTING THE CUSTOMER JOURNEY

I'll never forget staying at the TWA Hotel at JFK International Airport. It was like stepping back in time as I encountered staff dressed in the uniforms of the '70s, walked into displays of the common household of the '60s and '70s, and took a tour of one of their planes. I felt transported back to my childhood, and yet it also had a very modern vibe. What a perfect layover before heading on a journey overseas. The owners understand their audience and how to create a great experience.

If you're buying a loaf of bread off the shelves at your local supermarket, you have the right to expect the bread to be fresh, soft, and adequate for making sandwiches. But if you're buying artisanal bread, your expectations are much higher and more refined. Good bakers know what their audience wants and they meet those needs consistently.

If you've made it this far in the book, my assumption is that you're seeking to create a deeper, more personalized impact on your customers. You aren't looking to create a mass-appeal product with a cookie-cutter approach.

Instead, you seek to craft a unique journey for your customers that allows them to experience life-changing moments or at least shareworthy memories.

Asking questions

In the world of marketing, we often talk about a customer journey. The concept should also be applied to an event. Look at what people are doing at a given point in time, and ask yourself a few questions. Try to be detailed in your answers:

- What are they thinking right now?
- What are they feeling?
- What can they see, touch, and smell? What are those senses evoking for them?
- What could go wrong?
- How can we keep the journey going? What are the logical next steps?

Customer Service Cycle

John DiJulius, the creator of the Customer Service Revolution, taught me the importance of looking for service moments. He encouraged us to walk through our event from the viewpoint of an attendee. By doing this, we could identify all the key customer experiences. And *that* would show us service opportunities.

We created a list of things that might go wrong, such as at registration. We then asked ourselves two questions:

1. What is a standard level of service response?
2. What would it look like to go above and beyond?

The phrase "above and beyond" became our mantra. We now try to catch our volunteers and staff doing "above and beyond" acts of service. We give out buttons and coffee gift cards. Why? Because our customers tell us repeatedly about situations where something went wrong and how our staff came up with creative solutions.

The first step is to identify all the touch points within your event. Break it down to micro touch points. Then work your way through this grid by identifying potential problems. Come up with preemptive solutions, your on-site standard response, and your above-and-beyond response that you'll give whenever possible.

Example Grid: Getting to a Party

What Could Go Wrong:

Problem	Pre-Planning Solution	Standard Solution	Above & Beyond Solution
I can't find the shuttles.	Provide directional signage and strategically place staff.	Verbally direct guests to the bus location.	Staff walk attendees to the shuttle (no pointing).
I don't want to take the shuttle; I prefer to walk.	Provide printed walking directions.	Proactively give attendees a copy of the printed walking directions.	Staff members organize groups to walk to the party venue.
I'm not staying at the event hotel, so how do I get to the party?	Place information and directions on the website.	Strategically make staff available to provide directions in person and over the phone.	Have Uber/Taxi discount code or a complimentary coupon to hand out depending on circumstances.

It's a very worthwhile exercise to walk through your event agenda to identify potential customer service problems and how you can be prepared to solve them. Remember the story of the toothbrush? That's how we came up with that solution. We identified a problem. People would want to brush their teeth after a meal or at least have a mint to cover up any bad breath. We provided both. Our information desk keeps copious amounts of breath mints on hand, and our connections crew members carry them wherever they go. We also place toothbrushes, toothpaste, and mouthwash in the bathrooms.

In the wake of the global pandemic, some people had become less comfortable with personal hygiene items being left out in the open. What to do? We placed a card in the bathrooms inviting attendees to go to the info desk to get anything they needed. Few did, but all knew, and the thought mattered.

| **WARNING:** Be aware that some mouthwashes leave stain marks on the sinks. Test this in advance!

Context

You may or may not get to select the venue where you host your event. But just as the type of oven has a massive effect on the type of bread you bake, your venue influences how people experience your event. Hosting your event inside an airport convention center will feel very different from being in a nightclub, on a cruise ship, or at an art museum. Every venue wordlessly says something about your event.

If you have any level of control over choosing your venue, here are some questions to consider:

Location

Consider the geographic location of your event.

- Is this a desirable destination?
- Is it easy to get there for your attendees?
- Is it safe?

Capacity

This probably sounds obvious, but I can't tell you how many events end up with either too much space or too little.

- What's your projected attendance?
- What's the maximum attendance you expect at your largest sessions and parties?
- Will they comfortably fit?
- Are you willing to limit the attendance at your event to fit the venue?

Indoor/Outdoor

If your destination is desirable for going outside, does the venue allow for this? Do they have good solutions if the weather turns sour?

Vibe and culture

Ask your staff, customers, and stakeholders for their opinion. For example, if you're meeting in an artsy warehouse, but you're trying to appeal to a bunch of Wall Street investment bankers, does that convey what you want? Maybe or maybe not. If you're trying to challenge assumptions and look at things from a fresh perspective, meeting in a hotel conference room may not be the best choice—unless it's the TWA hotel in New York City!

- What does the venue say when you look at it?
- If your event is all about customer experience (which I assume is true, as you're reading this book), make sure you see evidence that it's true of the venue. Most hotels will nod their heads that customer service is a priority—after all, they are in the hospitality industry. But after doing a site visit and staying at their venue, you'll know immediately.
- Is your event dependent on good WiFi? If so, make sure the venue has a good solution or that you can bring in an outside solution. Don't brush over this. Our first year, we were convinced that the venue knew what they were talking about when it came to WiFi. They ended up having to eat part of a $50,000 bill because they failed to deliver the promised experience.

Labor and third-party vendors

Labor and third-party vendors represent your brand. You'll want to make sure they're a good fit.

- Will you be required to use a local labor union? This is good to know because it can have a material effect on your budget and the way you run the event.
- Will you be permitted to use a third-party vendor for catering, production, and other elements of your show? Or will you be required to use the internal provider or someone from a preferred list?
- If you're using union labor, be sure to understand rules about overtime, breaks, and meal penalties.

Costs and logistics

Here are some things to consider regarding budget, planning, and organization.

- What are all the projected costs? What are the costs for amendments? Can you make changes on-site and if so, what are the costs for doing so?
- Who will manage decisions about food and beverage if you run out of food or coffee?
- Do they charge for refilling the water stations?
- Do they charge extra if you have sponsors participating?
- Can you include sponsors who provide food or beverage? At what cost?
- How early can you set up, and how long do you have to move out?

Every one of these answers has a significant impact on the type of event you will run. This list isn't intended to be exhaustive but to get you thinking about the types of questions you should ask. All of these decisions have consequences.

Here's the good news: No matter what venue you select (or has been selected for you), you can influence that message through the use of graphics, furniture, lights, carpet, sound, and people. While you can never turn a cruise ship into a cavern, most event venues provide you with a canvas upon which you can paint the experience you desire.

> **The most important question:** Ask every vendor and venue this question: "What haven't I asked that I should be asking you?" That's when you'll get the hidden insights and information.

Environmental factors

Temperature and airflow have a profound impact on event experience. For instance, if the temperature gets too hot people will become lethargic and if it's too cold they will begin fidgeting to stay warm. It's impossible to please everyone's preferences for temperature when you're dealing with a geographically diverse audience. Northeners have a different tolerance for cold than Southerners, for instance.

Ventilation is something to pay attention to. Venues will show you how many seats fit in a room, but now how many people the ventilation system is designed to accommodate. It's well documented that at certain concentrations of atmospheric CO_2[15]—what we exhale—we experience substantial degradation of our mental faculties, and conferences (especially breakout rooms) routinely hit those numbers. Ask your event venues what the capacity of each room is for keeping CO_2 levels under 800 parts per million. They'll probably look at you like you're crazy, but it will give you some indication of whether they've even thought about this. More importantly, it will let you know if you should limit seating in the rooms.

Seasoning

In baking, the primary seasoning a baker uses is salt, but there are many others that can affect the outcome. These include cinnamon, nutmeg, or vanilla. Let's break down some of the event spices you can use and how they impact your event.

Colors

Color can have a profound, if unintended, impact on your event. Depending on things like age, ethnicity, and even the season of the year, the colors you choose for your graphics, lighting, and tablecloths can evoke different kinds of emotional responses. The intentional use of color can help reinforce the vibe you seek. You could also create emotional noise if the colors compete with the response you desire.

Here are some examples:

The color blue often evokes feelings of calming, soothing, trust, and loyalty. If, however, you have blue lighting immediately following lunch, you might as well hand out milk, cookies, and blankets because it will be nap time! (NOTE: I'm not discussing the blue light that emits from computers and cell phones. That presents it's own issues, but that's for a different book.)

Purple often represents royalty, wisdom, and wealth. Those would be great colors for a finance conference but probably not for an event advocating for the homeless.

Yellow creates a warm, cheery vibe if used sparingly. But if you use it too much, it becomes agitating.

Orange is a great color if you seek an atmosphere that is energetic, exciting, intense, and playful. It's often a better choice than red, which can evoke passion and excitement but also can be too intense or powerful. If your competitor's primary color is orange, you shouldn't emphasize it.

Branding experts[16] can help you really lean into the colors you should use. Be sure to choose an audio/visual company that understands how to use color to create the energy and mood you desire throughout your event.

> NOTE: If you are running an international event, keep in mind that colors mean different things in other parts of the world. For example, in the United States the color red typically is a sign of alarm and evokes a heightened state of alert. In China the color red can evoke pride and loyalty.

Layout

There are two facets to space design. One is the macro view where you look at how the rooms flow together and how the customer will experience the space. The second is more of a micro view where you look at seating, stages, and individual room experiences.

Once you've selected a venue, it's time to think about how you'll use it. Start to think through how your guests will experience the space. Here are some questions to ask:

- Where will people enter? Will they need to park?
- Where can you put the check-in or registration that will feel inviting and allow you to maintain good security?
- What's the best space to use for your main sessions? Does it have good capacity and people flow? How does it feel?
- Where will you hold different types of sessions, such as breakouts, if relevant?
- Where will you host meals and coffee? Where can people congregate to have informal conversations? Will you have a specific location for networking?
- Where can you place your sponsors so that they will get plenty of foot traffic and feel a natural part of the event?

- 🎂 Where will you put your offices and the speaker-ready room to be convenient and unobtrusive to the attendee experience?
- 🎂 Are there confusing parts of your venue where people might get lost? How will you solve this? Who will coordinate with venue staff to help with this?
- 🎂 How can you strategically use decorations to enhance the vibe you seek at the event? Decor can take a sterile conference room and turn it into an alternate reality.
- 🎂 Where are places in the event space that feel dead or uninviting? What kinds of things can you do to provide reasons for your guests to engage with each other or with aspects of your event?
- 🎂 What color carpet will you use? One year we had a whole debate online whether we should have blue or gray carpet in our exhibitor space. It was fun. If people are standing for long periods of time, doing so on concrete can be hard on the legs. Carpet can feel necessary, but it's also expensive to rent.
- 🎂 How can you limit the waste from your event? What recycling options do you have? Will the leftover food be sent to homeless shelters?

Seating

When it comes to user experience, the way you set a room has a tremendous impact. Traditional theater seating communicates that the focus is on the speaker and stage. Classroom-style seating with long tables and chairs says this is a serious learning event. If you seat people at round tables, it suggests that conversations are just as important as the presentation. Placing people in what event planners call chevron seating feels more open and inviting to the community, but it does limit the number of chairs you can put in a room.

Here are some standard seating arrangements for larger events (for pictures go to the website in this endnote[17]):

- 🎂 Chevron—angled sides to create a more communal feeling.
- 🎂 Auditorium/Theater—Traditional straight row seating.

- Banquet—Seating at round tables with 6 to 10 people per table. Often planners remove the chairs that have their backs to the stage, creating a semi-circle.
- Classroom—Seating at 6' or 8' tables allows for notetaking or use of computers. Sometimes planners will provide power drops (beware that this can get expensive if the venue requires you to pay for "power drops").

Many event organizers set rooms with a variety of seating types. You might find comfy couches up front, round tables in the middle, and standing tables in the back. This allows people to sit in the way that feels most comfortable. Again, this is expensive. Most venues only provide tables and chairs.

Note: If you change the way you set a room during the event, there is often a charge for this unless you are doing it to provide food.

Sound and lights

Sound and light design is one of your biggest costs and most important investments. If your attendees can't see or hear your speakers, people will complain. Here's the unfortunate truth: If the production company does their job perfectly, no one will notice or say anything. It's only when it's broken that people criticize. Your accountant may ask you why the production budget is so big if things go perfectly. You need to remember that it went perfectly because you selected the right company who took care of everything.

Let me shoot straight with you. There is no such thing as a perfect show. Something will always happen. A microphone will fail. A projector lamp will go out. A video will freeze up. The question is not only how to minimize these problems but what to do when it does happen.

A few things that are important, depending on the size of your show and budget:

- Do you plan to record? If so, find out how they handle backups. This is essential. Something always happens.
- Do you plan to livestream? If so, find out what services they are comfortable using.

- ♨ Do you plan to capture a video feed with your recordings? Find out how this works in union facilities. Often, it requires a whole extra person for each room.
- ♨ Do you plan to allow your speakers to video their own sessions? If so, find out how the production company prefers to handle this. Frequently, there are problems if the videographer wants to get an audio feed from the soundboard.
- ♨ Do you plan to have background music between sessions? If so, figure out who will provide it and how the list will get approved. Don't let a Spotify list just keep playing. It can eventually start to play suggested songs, and there may not be a filter for preventing songs with explicit lyrics.
- ♨ For larger shows, I highly recommend hiring a show caller/technical director. This person is worth their weight in gold. They will troubleshoot, find efficiencies, and show you ways to simplify and make your show even better.

Decorations

I mentioned a while ago that decorations can help you transform a venue. Let's talk for a minute about live versus artificial. Having live plants helps to better circulate oxygen in your space. It can help transform a sterile concrete room into a living environment. Your guests may not notice the difference. Not all of the plants have to be living, but it's worth having a couple of real palm trees brought in. Fake trees are pretty obvious, whereas plastic Ficus plants are less so.

The Water of Communication

When people travel to your event, they want to feel like they know what's going on. Intentional surprises are good, but keeping people in the dark about basic needs like food, water, and coffee forces people into survival mode. They will be less likely to engage in the deeper levels of your event.

One year, we underestimated how many people preferred their morning specialty coffee. Then we saw a line 100 people deep at the Starbucks store.

People were skipping sessions so they could have their morning pick-me-up. We had basic coffee available but grossly misunderstood how important specialty coffees would be for our audience.

Modes and degrees of delivery

Communication is the water your thirsty customers seek. You can choose how you will deliver the information they need. You can convey it via email, text, mobile app, signs, printed agendas, and even spoken announcements. Just be sure to have a plan. **Ideally, make sure your plan matches how your audience tends to consume information.**

Be aware that you have two general types of attendees: the zealous over-preparer and the go-with-the-flow attendee. The zealous types want as much information as they can get as early as possible. These are the ones for whom you'll send emails, prepare websites with lots of information, and even create downloadable PDFs. They will read it all and come ready. The go-with-the-flow types just want the information available when they need it. Your event app, program guide, and customer service team will be critical resources for these customers.

Different audiences

Most events under-communicate or only share some of the information. But it's possible to overcommunicate and still miss your audience. For instance, Comicon San Diego creates a 31-day countdown of tips for their event. As far as I know, this works great for them, but when we tried doing it, we discovered that our audience didn't even look at them. We wasted a lot of effort, and it yielded little fruit, even though it was fun.

Turns out that our audience isn't the same as Comicon. While we have strong fans, they aren't checking our website every day for announcements and updates.

Erin Gargan King used to run social media for the Oscars. She discovered a 90-day sweet spot for most event communication. Start ramping up your communication and social posting about 60 days pre-event. Keep it going for 30 days post-event.

Secret tip from Erin: Don't have the same team doing your social media before, during, and after the event. They will need a break. Have a staffing plan that allows for breaks and keeps people fresh.

Consistency across channels

I recommend organizing your communication so that you're consistent across all your channels. We compare our sales messages to see if paid attendees might want to receive announcements we are making to prospective customers. We also put it on a timeline so people are receiving information at the right time. This goes from our welcome sequence all the way through what we're sharing during and after the conference.

Sample Grid

Message	Email— Sales	Email— Attendee	Website	Attendee Portal	Social Media	Mobile App
Announce new speakers.	Send on 7/20.	Send on 7/20.	Add to speaker page 7/20.	Add a notice.	Share across Facebook, Twitter, and Instagram on 7/20.	n/a
Hotel rooms are running out.	n/a	Send on 8/31.	Add to hotel page.	Add a notice.	Share in Facebook group but not public pages.	Add notice to home screen.

Calendar Considerations

When constructing your agenda, there are many things to consider. It would be impossible to give you a step-by-step guide to the perfect agenda because events vary so greatly, but here are some principles to consider:

White space—Just as in art and in books, people need margin. Don't pack your event so full that people don't have time to breathe, think, or have a meaningful conversation. However, as your event grows, people will create their own agenda. You won't have to worry as much about this unless you have a single-track event.

Physical movement—The human body is designed to move, not sit for endless hours. Be sure to include ample breaks and insert opportunities to move. Some events will bring in a yoga instructor or a movement expert, like Lizzy Williamson, who does two-minute movement activations.

Choose your own adventure—This may be the most important principle when it comes to calendar planning. Mentally walk several different attendee avatars through the event. See if it's easy for them to make the choices that are best for their learning and networking objectives. This is much like designing a video game. People get overwhelmed if you give them too many choices at once. They will keep making progress if you limit the options to two or three at a time. On a piece of paper, you might draw a decision tree and watch where it leads.

Make your agenda easy to read—The more complex your event, the more important it is to have an easy-to-decipher code for discovering agenda options. Color coding and even having icons can help. Keep it consistent between your print guide (if you have one) and your website, mobile app, and on-site signage.

Impact

"Do for one what you wish you could do for everyone."
−Andy Stanley

No two customers will experience your event in the exact same way. There may be some predictable patterns. You should plan for those and allow for personalization. The clearer your customers are on their goals, the easier it will be for them to plan their experience. Make the options clear.

Some of the choices you make won't be overtly noticed by your customers. You may even have team members who question your decisions about seating, lighting, or color. But these choices make a subconscious impact on the customer's experience. Be aware of which seem to impact your customers the most. Make sure you remove your personal bias and look for data to support your conclusions.

One year, we were looking into methods for adding certain aromas to our event. There are some very cool technologies available for doing this at scale, but they also require rental fees that are many thousands of dollars. We could purchase essential oil diffusers for much less and place them in strategic locations. It made a dramatic impact. We observed people relax when they got to our registration desks, so we kept this practice and never made the larger investment.

Bread Bite

Just as great bakers keep experimenting with their recipes until they get them right, you may have to experiment and/or adjust as your event experiences changes year after year.

Question: What is the coolest event space you've seen? What is the worst? Why do you think they were different? How did they impact your experience?
Exercise: Create a storyboard of your customer's ideal event journey. Create a picture of each significant step and describe what is happening. What are they thinking, feeling, and doing? What are you and your team doing? Describe the setting. What changes could you make (good and bad) at each stage that will impact the user experience? Highlight the ideal choices that will create the optimal experience. Discuss with your team how that is different or the same as what you expected.

Section III:

Creating Your Own Recipe

Chapter 12:

HOW TO CREATE YOUR RECIPE

I'll never forget Mr. Wong. He owned a small hole-in-the-wall Vietnamese restaurant in Littleton, Colorado. The food was good and affordable, but the experience was unrivaled. He always remembered my name and spent a good five minutes giving me a hard time about being single and good looking. He made us all feel like family. You can imagine his surprise when I eventually brought my wife to meet him. Now I was ugly and she was beautiful!

So far in this book, we've talked about all the ingredients needed to create a memorable experience. I've intentionally resisted the temptation to give you a recipe. Here's why:

If you were a twelve-year-old or just getting started running events, a recipe would be a helpful place to start, but it would never lead you to create something memorable. Instead, you would be recreating someone else's memorable event.

I've been part of quite a few church plants (new churches). There's always a temptation to copy what someone else is doing. In the late '90s, many churches started copying Willow Creek Community Church, a megachurch in the Chicago suburbs. I was part of a church that sought to do that. It never really took off until we let go of those training wheels and created our own vision.

Checklists and processes are valuable. And benefiting from someone else's procedures will save you time. But make sure you know why you're doing certain things. Remember the bakery I mentioned where the head baker couldn't answer my questions about why she made the bread the way she did? She was part of a franchise. She didn't necessarily need to know all the whys.

Most likely, you aren't creating a franchise event that will happen dozens of times a year. If you are, it's even more important that you think through every element of your recipe to ensure consistency and allow for adaptability.

In short, create your own checklists. Develop them for remembering all the steps and procedures you've figured out. We make use of project management tools and process documenting tools for this very reason.

At one of our conferences, we had a high turnover rate on our team. While the new team had lots of event experience, they didn't have experience with *our* event. As a result, some of our checklists appeared to be unnecessary or overkill. They ignored them. We ended up regretting it because those checklists were invented to ensure we remembered important elements of the event.

Recipes are important. But create your own recipe as soon as you can.

Here's what I know: If I give you and five other event organizers the same recipe for creating an event, all of your events will turn out differently. You can't help it because you will approach it as you. That's appropriate. I want you to figure out how to put your personality and approach into the event while also creating a memorable experience for your customers.

Steps to a Memorable Experience

Let's review the steps:

1. **Start with your customer**. Get to know your customers. What do they like? What do they need? How can you create a memorable experience for them? Have they been to your events before? What expectations do they have?

2. **Prepare your crew**. Get your staff, volunteers, and vendors all on the same page. If you don't have the right chefs in the kitchen, so to speak, you will be frustrated all along the way.

3. **Select your content carefully**. At learning events, the sessions and workshops are the primary reason people attend. Take your time in choosing the topics and experts, as this is how people will judge and remember your event. Look for experts who will invest in the community.

4. **Focus on connections**. People travel to events because they want to learn together. Make that easy. Find a group of super-connectors who will disperse within the event like yeast and engage attendees in conversation with the goal of making some helpful introductions. Your parties, breaks, and space should all make it easy for your customers to meet each other.

5. **Dial in the conditions for change**. Your venue, mindset, and approach can all create the potential for serendipitous moments.

6. **Culture matters**. People can feel the culture of your event. It's a combination of all the things above, but it's also how you go about customer service and the mindset/attitude of your staff.

7. **Walk in your customer's shoes**. The customer journey is your ultimate test. If you create an awesome experience, but no one ever participates, you'll have failed. Anticipate and predict where and how your customer will participate so you can create the right experience.

Formulating Your Recipe

Josh Allen, the baker, taught us that once we are clear on what our customer wants to taste (experience), we can begin experimenting until we get our recipe and process down. If you only do one event per year, this experimentation process can take time. If you run dozens of events per year, you'll learn much faster. But even those of us who do very few events can learn by watching other events and joining the volunteer team for those events.

Testing

A good scientist knows that you have to be able to measure the results of your actions. That requires you to isolate your actions as much as possible. Then you'll be able to tell what kind of impact they had. The process starts by creating and testing a hypothesis.

When it comes to your event, I encourage you to come up with a statement on each of these major ingredients. Get your team to meet with you to describe and assess your current event based on each one of these criteria.

Once you've described your condition, come to a consensus on which aspects of the event might need to change the most to create the experience your customer desires. Once you identify that category, come up with a list of ten ways you might address that needed change. Don't prejudge your ideas. Normally, it will take you a while to brainstorm your best ideas. Some bad ideas need to be generated before the good ones emerge.

Narrow your list of ten down to one or two that are worth trying. Select one. Create an experiment around that idea. State the experiment in a way you'll know whether it had the intended consequence or not. Then test it. Make sure you have a way to capture data to find out if it worked. Put someone in charge of the experiment. If no one owns it, no one will know if it worked.

One at a time

You can run multiple experiments at once, but recognize that each may affect the outcome of the others. For example, you might run two experiments related to content and connections simultaneously. You can't completely isolate them. As a result, you won't know whether the content experiment truly improved the content experience, or if the connections experiment also impacted those results.

If you have a brand-new event, this whole process will be easier because you can describe and create the ideal experience for your customer without concern for history. I still recommend that you document your theory and have ways to test whether it worked.

Remember that you aren't the judge of whether your experiments worked. Your customers are. Take time to listen to them through surveys and conversations.

Becoming a master baker

The best event designers learn to master their craft through constant experimentation and study. They also learn from their peers at industry events and by working on the staff of other events.

When I started in music ministry, a mentor challenged me to regularly participate in musical ensembles where I wouldn't be in charge. Play in the pit orchestra for a musical. Sing in a community choir. Play saxophone in someone else's band. His rationale was that I would notice things I could implement (or avoid) in my own work.

A fast track to mastery is to find a small group of mentors and peers who will push and challenge you. If you watch shows like *Iron Chef* on the Food Network, you can see how elite chefs learn from each other.

Jim Rohn said that you're the average of the five people you spend the most time with. Build a list of fellow event organizers who can push you, but also create a list of five mentors you can study from afar and maybe eventually get to know. Then watch them.

I've been telling you about some of mine throughout this book, but there's one person I want to celebrate and memorialize how she impacted me.

A Tribute to Tracey Brouillette

My friend Tracey Brouillete passed away from cancer in late 2021. She was an assistant sales director at the Hilton San Diego Bayfront, but she became a friend because she knew how to treat people like family. I didn't think of her as a supplier or vendor but as a friend. In fact, I attended and officiated her memorial service because I cared for her and the community that loved her. Her family saw that and asked me to lead the service.

I have many memories with Tracey, but two experiences stand out that illustrate well the power of memorable experiences.

A Padre baseball game

In 2015, Tracey took me and a few friends to a San Diego Padre baseball game. I had attended a game before with my kids, but they were too young to enjoy the game, so we left before the seventh-inning stretch.

The experience with Tracey was vastly different. I don't remember who the Padres played or who won. I do remember the food and getting our pictures on the Megatron screen. Tracey left every inning to grab us enough food to feed an army. By the fifth inning, we were all stuffed, but when she invited us to dinner after the game, we could hardly say no.

Notice what I remember: Tracey's hospitality and being noticed. Even my boss saw us on the big screen and commented.

But Tracey's hospitality stood out more than anything else. She didn't want us to have a bad experience, so she kept bringing food and drinks and ensuring that we were taken care of. She didn't even watch the game. One of her colleagues commented that Tracey sacrificed her personal well-being for the benefit of her clients, colleagues, and family. That's what great hosts do.

In the best sense of the stereotype, she felt like the mother who keeps bringing great food out and saying, "Eat. Eat. There's plenty more. You boys need to be strong."

That was the day I cemented a friendship with Jason, Jeff, and Eric. To this day, we are in a weekly men's group. I doubt that group would have started if not for the experience Tracey created for us.

I remember the food from that game not because it was amazing, but because it was abundant and a bit unusual. We had barbeque ribs, spicy sunflower seeds, and craft beer. My salt and savory senses had a feast that day. Of course, I needed to go running for a week to feel like I had run it all off.

What can we learn?

Hospitality and service are key ingredients for great experiences. Good hosts are very attentive to the needs of their guests. They anticipate and satisfy needs before they're even mentioned. Tracey left every inning to get drinks and food so that we wouldn't have to leave the game. She wanted us to enjoy the game. I know she was an avid baseball fan, but that night, she was a fan of my friends and me. It felt great.

Creating space for conversations leads to lasting memories. In this particular instance, I remember the conversations with my new friends more than the ones with Tracey. She was a facilitator of connections. I invited those guys because I knew we had a few things in common. I even worked with Jeff and Erik at the time, but I wanted to get to know them more, and a baseball game seemed like a good place for that.

If you show up, serendipity will happen. I don't think Tracey arranged for our faces to get on the Megatron screen, but we were in good, visible seats, and it would have never happened if we hadn't attended. Then again, it wouldn't surprise me to learn that Tracey had a connection with the A/V team and asked them to look for us at some point during the game. Regardless, we showed up, and Tracey kept us engaged with the game and each other. That's when the serendipity of a special moment and lasting relationships developed.

Juniper and Ivy

A lingering conversation at Juniper and Ivy led to a meaningful moment. A couple of years later, Tracey asked if she and her boss, Andy Paschke, could take me to dinner while I was on a site visit. I said sure, as long as my daughter could join us. Tracey gladly agreed and made reservations at Juniper and Ivy. I had never heard of it, but was I in for a treat!

Juniper and Ivy advertises itself as "refined American dining." From the valet parking to the maitre d' to the extensive wine list, the restaurant spoke of sophistication and elegance. We enjoyed a memorable culinary experience, but that only set the table (puns intended always) for the conversation that followed.

I'm a meat-and-potatoes guy from Kansas. I don't need a fancy restaurant to feel special, but Tracey made us feel very special that night.

I know from Tracey's perspective this was coincidental, but it's fitting that it happened with her in this specific context. Earlier that year, I had a revelation about the power of stretching time or what I call "making time stand still." I knew I had a book idea brewing, and I wanted to talk with Tracey and her boss, Andy, about this.

In the context of superb service, we discussed how hotels and restaurants create an environment where powerful memories and meaningful moments are created. We discussed the importance of customer service, space design, and event flow. Talk about a metanarrative!

I remember vividly remarking about how one of their competitor hotels impressed me deeply one year, but over time, the service levels had declined.

It made me less inclined to hang out at that hotel, which would cause me to leave prematurely and perhaps miss an important meetup.

That conversation was where I first noticed the power of hyper-personalization and the merry-go-round principle.

> The **merry-go-round principle** says that events try to give you a memorable ride, but if things move too slowly, you'll want to get off. If it moves too quickly, you'll be given a memorable ride, but it will make you sick. The perfect merry-go-round ride gives you a thrill without throwing you off or making you sick. It's similar to an ideal event or restaurant experience.

We lingered over dinner for three to four hours. Once again, Tracey kept ordering food and drinks for us to try. The waiter knew how to keep adding layers to our experience without inserting himself into our conversation (though his service was noticed). The bill was not small that night, but the value of the conversation far exceeded the price of the meal.

What can we learn?

Context matters. This powerful memory would not be nearly as rich had we met at Denny's or McDonald's. From the menu to the wait staff to the interior design, everything invited us to have a deep conversation. We didn't want to leave when our meal was over.

Service triumphs over glitz. While Ivy and Juniper is an upscale restaurant, the elegance is understated. It's the people who shine. I recall from the valet to the maitre d' to the waiter, we received amazing service all evening long.

Stay curious. Andy and Tracey both asked lots of questions and shared examples from their experience of how the merry-go-round principle plays out in a hotel. Their curiosity sparked my own questions. The conversation stands out in my memory and Andy's five years later.

An unexpected unconventional moment

We learned earlier that Tracey loved baseball and was the consummate host. At her memorial service, those themes kept arising as each friend and family member shared their eulogies.

When it was my turn to share some final thoughts and bring the service to a close, I knew there were two things I would do. First, I shared a song I wrote about Tracey. That song was a tearjerker. In fact, I refused to perform it live because I knew I would cry. When the song finished, I knew exactly what Tracey would do at that moment.

If Tracey had been alive with so many friends and family members gathered, she would have ordered a bus and taken everybody to a Padres baseball game. With that in mind, I did something I likely will never do again at a memorial service. I pulled out my saxophone and led everybody in the quintessential American baseball song, "Take Me Out to the Ball Game."

When people left, they were saying it was the best memorial service they've ever attended. I don't think that's necessarily true, but I made it deeply personal. Between the songs and the stories, people felt like they had one final experience with their friend that was deeply meaningful and highly memorable. There is no replacement for the power of memory, meaning, and moments.

The Essential Ingredients

As we've discussed, the essential event ingredients include content, conversations, connections, and context. Choices about decor, color, lighting, agenda, and more are like spices.

Thinking about these experiences with Tracey, I see all these key ingredients at play. The content was the experience (a Padres game or a dinner). Conversations were rich. New connections were created, and old connections were deepened through curiosity. And the contexts were selected for their ability to create the space for memorable experiences.

Mixing the Ingredients

I'm not much of a baker, but I watched my mother and grandmother enough to know things have to be mixed in the right order. You wouldn't blend the frosting with the flour, for instance.

When planning events, it's easy to forget the essential ingredients and obsess over the frosting and decorations. Those make the dessert unique, but unless you have a great batter, they don't matter much. If you do have a great cake, you rarely need a lot of extras.

Many events have had to be reinvented. Budgets were scrapped and recreated, forcing organizers and planners to rethink what makes a great event. If we're going back to the basics, make sure it looks something like this formula:

(Conversations + Connections) * Choices = Memorable Experiences

Conversations include expert content, organized discussions, and informal meetings. Great events create space for all of these and facilitate them naturally. Often the magic allows for the seamless continuation of dialogue between different levels of conversation.

If you have to choose between people and technology or design elements, always go with people. Cool graphics and innovations will get their attention, but it's how people feel that will stand the test of time. Only people can make the kinds of impact you want to create. That includes customer service and the power of community.

Yeast is a super-agent. It only takes one or two parts per hundred to cause bread to rise. At events, yeast represents the super-connectors—the people who love meeting and introducing people. Empower your connectors to connect and spread throughout the event. If yeast clumps up, it won't cause the whole community to rise.

Curiosity: the Unstoppable Superpower

Not many people are super-connectors, but everyone can remain curious. Encourage your staff and attendees to stay present and remain interested. I firmly believe this: "Everyone has a story worth hearing." My corollary is "And nothing tells a story like a song."

What if most people attending your event had the mindset of an 1848 California gold digger? They'd come hungry to discover the gold. At events, we can discover that gold becomes more valuable when it's shared.

Did you notice that both experiences I shared about Tracey highlighted the importance of customer service and the role of space? It's just like the baker who has the right ingredients and the right experience. You give the same ingredients to an inexperienced baker, and the results could be terrible. Likewise, if you give mediocre ingredients to a master baker, you'll still get a great cake or loaf of bread.

Great events need event staff who follow the mantra, "Listen carefully. Respond creatively." This idea stems from Darren Ross, the CEO of Magic Castle Hotel. Some call him the Chief Executive Freak because he's so freakish about customer service. His attention to detail led him to say, "Treating guests with warmth and respect while anticipating their needs will go a long way toward earning their loyalty."

Great service agents know how to listen carefully. They aren't just listening to the words. They are studying the body language and responding creatively to what they notice.

David Wagner used to work for the Customer Service Revolution. One year, he noticed that an attendee he was speaking with becoming pale. He stopped her and asked if she was feeling well.

She said she felt faint and asked for some water and a place to rest.

As David helped her, he realized she was in a health crisis. He rushed her to a hospital.

By paying attention and taking action David may have literally saved her life. That is more than probably 98% of event leaders would ever do. (It's not that other event managers don't care. We just might not have noticed she was in crisis.)

But David kept serving. As she was admitted to the hospital, he decided to stay with her—for two days.

Can you imagine your primary event director not being available during your big annual conference for two days?

We could argue whether David was the right person to do that, but he demonstrated above-and-beyond customer service. That lady will never forget, and I'll bet you won't, either.

Bread Bite

Experiments and experience will help you create your own recipe for your events. Remember Tracey Brouillette and the way she met people's needs, and you'll do well.

Question: Have you ever created your own recipe for a food dish? How did that process work for you? How can you relate that experience to creating your own recipe(s) for the event you run?

Exercise: Get your team together for 90 minutes and work through the steps in this chapter for creating your current event recipe. Then identify what change will have the biggest positive change on your event. Also note which element, if removed, would most dramatically impact your event negatively. Decide on one experiment you will conduct at your next event.

Chapter 13:

BECOMING UNIQUE:
WHAT IF EVERYONE SANG YOUR SONG?

I'll never forget the first time we did a musical parody at our conference. I asked Amy Landino to be Dorothy and a few other speakers and attendees to fill out the cast. Lisa Rothstein (the illustrator in this book) wrote the story and lyrics. We kept it a secret so that not even the CEO knew what was happening. Right after his opening keynote I came out to make an announcement, but instead said that I asked some friends to help me make the announcement. After a short 10-minute sketch the house stood in applause and I heard afterword that it was one of the boldest and innovative things they've ever seen at a business conference. Turns out industrial musicals[18] have been done for a while.

Singing at the Table?

Does your family allow singing at the table? When's the last time you sang at a business meeting you attended? What about at your events?

Growing up, we weren't allowed to sing at the table—or hum or whistle, for that matter. It went against all rules of etiquette. I didn't question it at the time. Now, I wonder who decided that rule?!

While there's growing research and trends showing the benefits of singing at work and in all of life, we still tend to relegate singing to culturally accepted places and times.

It's time to change that. I believe we can all benefit from more singing. And who knows? Music could be just the thing that makes your event different.

The Neuroscience of Singing

Science is starting to reveal enormous mental benefits from singing. Singing changes your brain by lowering stress, reducing anxiety, and elevating endorphins. Research shows that singing can also increase your immune response, improve sleep, increase your pain tolerance, and help you feel more connected.

> "The neuroscience of singing shows that when we sing, our neurotransmitters connect in new and different ways. It fires up the right temporal lobe of our brain, releasing endorphins that make us smarter, healthier, happier, and more creative. When we sing with other people, this effect is amplified."
> —Cassandra Sheppard

Researchers for the *Oxford Handbook of Music* show that singing "requires the concerted effort of a vast network of brain regions." Intentional training and development enhance these networks—improving performance, creativity, and happiness.

Event Insight #1: Better State of Mind

Music puts people in a better state of mind to learn and to be open to new experiences.

Andy Sharpe is CEO of Song Division, a company that hires studio musicians to create unique musical experiences at conferences of all sizes, up to 50,000 people. He shared that live music is better than prerecorded music, but it's best when the music is participatory.

Song Division goes to conferences to help teams of people write and perform original songs based around themes generated at the conference. It taps into their creativity, gets people working together, and allows participants to let out their inner rock star. At the end of the experience, each team performs their song backed up by a professional band.

Andy observed that these experiences noticeably change the atmosphere. Sometimes they are asked to create this experience when two companies are merging as the result of a hostile takeover. People are fearful and resentful as they enter the room. But this musical experience allows people to express themselves and sets the stage for the hard conversations needed.

If you're like many people I know, you may not be convinced that you should intentionally include music. Isn't a DJ good enough?

Let's consider some other factors.

Part of our lives

Singing is part of our lives. Think about all the places in our lives where we sing. As a former worship pastor, I know that singing is a huge part of church gatherings. The Bible clearly teaches us to sing all kinds of songs—songs of praise, thanksgiving, and lament.

But singing isn't just for church.

We sing at birthday parties and karaoke bars, where it's expected to be offkey and obnoxious. Most of us feel comfortable singing in the shower, in the car, and at concerts—as long as no one can hear us.

Singing *The National Anthem* at sporting events is commonplace. And we love to sing and shout for joy when our team wins. Queen's song, "We Are the Champions," will live on because we all love to be winners.

We expect singing at funerals. "Amazing Grace" may be the most popular song in human history just because of how many times it's been sung at gravesides.

Singing at work

For certain types of work, singing is also very normal. Sailors sing sea chanties. Some became popular because of the movie *Fisherman's Friends* and the rage on TikTok whereby a man received a record deal. Slaves sang spirituals. Soldiers chant while they run, and factory workers whistle while they work.

But for most of us, the only songs we hear at work are the jingles written to promote our brand or the quiet Muzak playing in the background. Think of a jingle for a product or company you love. Can you hear the song? "Ba-da-ba-ba-ba. I'm loving it."

Why don't more white-collar workers sing on the job? I find it curious that singing is more commonplace in certain parts of society and in some cultures than others. When I spent seven months in Kenya, the plantation workers there sang while they walked and played and when they gathered after work. But I don't think I've ever been in a business meeting in the US where we were encouraged to sing anything but "Happy Birthday."

Why do you think that is?

At our annual conference, Social Media Marketing World, in 2015, I decided to run an experiment. I wanted to see if marketers would sing in a choir. I was surprised to see as many as 100 people signing up each year to sing. They told me that it gave them great joy to sing and use their musical gifts.

One of the reasons we don't sing at work is because we think it's inappropriate or unproductive. What if I told you singing could help release your best ideas, improve teamwork, and reduce turnover?

I've run many experiments like this. We were trying to come up with some new ideas at work for a future product launch. To get my brain flowing, I decided to sit down at the piano and play and sing for a few minutes. I knew the research shows that music accesses parts of the brain we don't normally use in everyday thought and conversation. I wanted to see what would happen.

After only 10 minutes of playing and singing, I pulled out pen and paper and started looking at the data with fresh eyes. I filled 5 sheets of paper with ideas and thoughts in less than 20 minutes. I'm a creative person—some call me an idea factory—but even I was astonished at how many ideas I generated.

While my experience is anecdotal, Duncan Wardle, former Head of Innovation & Creativity at Disney, says, "When asked, the majority of people always tell me they get their best ideas in the shower. They will also tell you it's the only place they ever sing. Coincidence?"

Film Scores

Have you ever watched a familiar movie without the sound? It's not nearly as impactful. You might know the story and the dialogue, but the music and sound effects transform the experience. There's a reason why John Williams and Hans Zimmer get paid enormous sums to write the scores that match the dialogue down to the second.

In speaking to event musicologist John Vitale, he suggested that event organizers approach their conferences and events with the same mindset as a film score composer. Instead of plotting out each second, he encourages us to think about each scene or block of time. The goal is to curate the experience to go with the natural emotional journey.

> **"Event producers often leave music as a last-minute item for their A/V provider to figure out. Why do that? Music is one of the most effective ways to connect emotionally with the attendees and supercharge each module of a show."**
> —John Vitale, Event Musicologist and Founder, Brain Music Labs

For instance, look at the circadian rhythms. Our moods, energy, and motivation are different in the morning, noon, and night. The music we play should match this and compliment the state of mind we want people to achieve to maximize learning, networking, creating, or deep thinking.

Where do you start? It's not with your favorite band or genre. The foundation is rhythm. The faster the beat the more agitated people will get. You probably want to create a relaxed environment in the 80 bpm range (just 10–20 bpm above the average resting heartrate of your audience).

Once you know the tempo range you want, then think about the psychographics of your audience. If you know your audience ranges in age from 25–65, but the majority are between the ages of 35–45 and North American women you can start to look at the kinds of music they likely listened to when they were between the ages of 12–22. In those younger years they might associate the songs with being happy and those older years they might associate with wanting to change the world. What emotion are you trying to tap into?

One of the biggest mistakes event organizers make when it comes to music is to just hand music selection to their Audio/Visual Production company without giving insights or guidance. What most audio engineers will do in that situation is say, "Do you want 80s or 90s music?" Then they'll find a playlist and forget about it. What can happen then is the wrong song comes on that pulls peoples' minds out of the event and to listening to the music.

Another mistake you can make is to have too many songs with lyrics. I'm not suggesting you play all classical or jazz music, unless that's the right genre for your event. Instead, take the songs from the right genre and time period and get a band to play cool instrumental versions. Or get a DJ to find instrumental arrangements that match the vibe you're looking for. Here's the reason: song lyrics can create a secondary dialogue in people's brains that is counter to your goal. There are times for lyrical songs that advance the flow of your event, but it can just as easily undermine your event.

If you don't know how to do this, consider hiring a music supervisor or a DJ who can understand your event goals and create the right plan to enhance the entire mental and emotional journey of your attendees.

> **WARNING:** Don't just choose your personal preference in music. Even if you're part of the target audience, make sure you get outside confirmation that you're hitting the sweet spot. Music can be very personal and it's hard to see our biases."

Event Insight #2: Our Inner Child

Our first year of Social Media Marketing World, we decided to host a karaoke night. We weren't sure if anyone would show up. Indeed, the lines were short at the beginning, but once a few speakers got onstage, dozens of people signed up. We were having friendly fights as people tried to get onstage. Someone even tried to bribe me to get moved up on the list!

Why?

People love being seen and heard. Singing is a great way to bring out our inner child.

Inhibitions

Not everyone enjoys singing. Some avoid it because it makes them feel awkward. They may not have a strong voice, know the song, or find it easy enough to sing.

I spent over 25 years serving churches as a worship leader. I've seen countless people—especially men—fold their arms while we sang as if to say, "I dare you to make me sing."

We might also be afraid our song will be heard online.

A viral video: the real story

I'm internet famous. I never wanted to be, but it happened. Well, I joked about going viral and getting famous, but I wouldn't wish this kind of fame on anyone—not even my enemies.

In 2014, I wrote a song for our conference because that's what I enjoy doing. I was attempting to be funny, but I learned a hard lesson: I'm not that funny. I've since made the decision to cowrite nearly every song that I write. And cowriting is a beautiful example of how music creates bonds and taps into our collective creativity.

The song was called, "Let's Get Social." I asked a participant to sing the song because I knew my voice couldn't carry it. Unfortunately, I didn't ask her to perform it as a comical song, so it came off as serious, and then I made a fatal decision to rap. Let's just say my rap skills are fine for a youth summer camp where it's meant to be a parody, but millions of people have now let me know that I should leave rapping to the experts.

I released the song on my personal channel after the conference because we didn't have a business YouTube account at that time. Within days, it started going viral. People began attacking our company and me. It hurt because it was so misunderstood, but it didn't change my conviction that music plays an important role at conferences.

Nor did it ultimately thwart my desire to create original theme songs for our conference. Instead, I resolved that we would always have really great songs and that the performers would be outstanding. That's also when we first introduced a choir.

We've written some really great songs and worked with award-winning songwriters from San Diego, Los Angeles, Atlanta, and Nashville.

I know that not everyone enjoys our original theme songs or the musicals we've performed (more on that in a minute), but it's part of what makes us unique. Live music is part of our signature.

Encouraging Singing at Events

How might we encourage singing at events? First, sing people's praises. Celebrate birthdays, special accomplishments, or milestones. Put it to a song that everyone can sing.

Second, come up with a theme song that everyone will learn and sing together. The Savannah Bananas include the song, "Hey, Baby," three different times at their events. By the third time, everyone is on their feet doing the dance and singing, even if they don't know the song.

Third, consider forming an event choir. Companies like Google, Facebook, Boeing, and LinkedIn have started forming choirs due to the health, social, and mental benefits. Lindsay Dempsey is the founder of EllaVate (formerly known as Sing at Work), and she has seen a tremendous benefit to employees who rediscover their voice as they sing together at work and conferences. At our conference, I heard trained musicians who are now marketers tell me that they never saw the way to combine their skills until they sang in our choir.

Lindsay is a trained opera singer. Her team worked with the CEO of a company who delivered his annual vision by putting it into an operatic recitative. His employees were impressed, and it became an unforgettable, highly shareable moment.

Fourth, look at your talent pool, and see what's possible. In 2015, I noticed that we had quite a few people with musical theater backgrounds and one person who had written copy on Madison Avenue and loved writing lyrics for musicals. We decided to try a parody based on *The Wizard of Oz*. It brought the house down. We kept doing it for the next five years.

Another thing we saw is that there were quite a few former professional musicians in our midst. We decided to form an All-Star band that allowed these musicians to come together for a couple of songs.

Bread Bite

By all means, allow singing at the table—and at our events. Let's get rid of the social stigma that singing shouldn't be allowed at the table. Of course, there's a time and place. Breaking out into "Let It Go" while someone is talking might be rude, but then again, it might be exactly what they need to hear!

Question: How might you incorporate more music and singing into your event?
Exercise: Think through what it could look like. Make a list of people you already know who might be able to facilitate it.

Chapter 14:

BECOMING THE ONLY ONE: FINDING YOUR SECRET INGREDIENT

I'll never forget the challenge of learning the McDonald's jingle back in the '70s. Do you remember their advertisement for the Big Mac? I still remember it 50 years later.

Doesn't the phrase "special sauce" make you wonder what's in it?

My daughter recently started working for a local restaurant. One of their featured menu items is chicken wings, but they invented their own version of Buffalo sauce. They call it Augustine sauce. The name created enough intrigue that we had to ask about it. Guess what? It's a secret recipe!

In the 1940s and '50s, the Waldorf-Astoria hotel owned a secret recipe for red velvet cake. Legend has it that a guest asked for the recipe and the chef sent it to her along with a bill for $350. She was so upset that she shared it with everyone she knew, including a bus full of random people. That's how my grandmother came to possess the recipe, and it became our annual birthday cake. It's no longer a secret recipe, but I'm pretty sure they held something back when it comes to how they make the frosting. But my grandmother and mother solved that with copious amounts of butter! Yum!

Are you salivating yet? Your secret sauce or ingredient should whet the appetite of your audience.

Have you noticed how many people claim to have the answer on how to stand out in a busy world? Most of them are just teaching you to be a little bit better, louder, or different from your competition. You're essentially still playing the same game. It's like prepackaged bread companies competing with each other. It's all bread, but none of them can compete with a high-quality loaf of artisan bread.

Making a New Category

Your goal is to create a whole new category. Srinivas Rao wrote the book, *Unmistakable: Why Only is Better Than Best*. He says it's like we're all zebras. Yes, every zebra has a different stripe pattern, but do you really want to try to stand out in a herd of zebras? It's far better to be a giraffe in a zeal of zebras (yes, a zeal is another word for a herd specifically applied to zebras).

Remember Jesse Cole and the Savannah Bananas? They don't see themselves competing with baseball teams. They realize they are an entertainment company, but they have no direct competitors. Who else can say they are "Harlem Globetrotters meets WWE on a baseball field with a dash of Disney and Steve Jobs"?

Jesse's mission is to do things in every game that have never been done on a baseball field before, for the sake of entertaining his fans.

What can you do in your business that puts you in a whole different category? Here are some suggestions to get you started:

#1: Understand your competition.

Most of us get caught up comparing ourselves to the closest competitors in our industry. That's not necessarily bad, but it's not the best place to look for inspiration. If we only focus on beating our competitors, we may still lose. And who are our competitors, anyway?

I'm in the event space, so let's use that industry as an example.

In April 2020, virtual events started to boom. While we've been doing virtual events since 2009, all of a sudden, people were becoming Virtual Event Experts with certifications. We've all attended far too many virtual events. While we don't enjoy them, they are here to stay in some form or another. One of our competitors is virtual events.

But we're also competing with all forms of entertainment. Whether it's movies, concerts, sporting events, or YouTube and TikTok videos, our customers are looking for distraction, entertainment, and education in all kinds of places. As a result, they've grown accustomed to high-quality production and entertainment value.

Martin Fretwell runs a company called Fyrelite that decided to zig when everyone else was zagging. Instead of trying to create bigger and bigger events, he decided to focus on making intimate networking dinners with very select groups of people. He creates a fabulous experience with carefully selected food and thoughtfully orchestrated conversations. His customers, who tend to be high-powered C-level executives, rave about his events and keep returning. Martin makes the case that your goal shouldn't be to compete but to do your own thing.

#2: Look for inspiration in unexpected places.

How much of your time is spent reading and watching material from outside your industry? I challenge you to shake it up. Spend at least 30% of your time studying subjects that have nothing to do with your profession. Everything is connected. You may find your best ideas develop in that process.

> **"I do not wish the ordinary reader to read no modern books.**
> **But if he must read only the new or only the old, I would advise him to read the old."**
> —C.S. Lewis

Since discovering the power of the baking metaphor for this book, I've met with at least five bakers. Each one of them has inspired me and given me insights I never would have discovered on my own. I have a whole new respect for the craft of baking and what goes into it.

You may wonder where you should look for inspiration. Follow your curiosity. If you're interested in something, become a student of that subject or person. For example, Jesse Cole finds Walt Disney to be a great source of inspiration. As a result, he has read every book he could and interviews people who knew Walt whenever he gets the chance.

Where else can you look for inspiration? Everyone looks at people like Walt Disney, PT Barnum, and Steve Jobs for creative inspiration. I encourage you to find unexpected sources. And if you're up to a challenge, find one source that was written at least 100 years ago and one source from a culture completely different from your own.

We live in a world where an idea that is six months old is outdated, but the kinds of inspiration you seek don't live in those constraints. People have been creating experiences since the first campfire.

#3: Combine the known to create the unknown.

While there's really nothing new under the sun, we can combine things in unique ways that create a whole new category. For example, consider the game of pickleball. It's really just a combination of ping pong, tennis, and badminton with some fun rules. I grew up with a Sport Court in our backyard and could have played pickleball for decades, but I thought it was a kid's game. I didn't take it seriously. Now I'm learning of professionals who are making a living from playing pickleball tournaments! Talk about a whole new category.

In 2016, I noticed that we had quite a few speakers and industry leaders who had strong music theater backgrounds. We decided to create a miniature parody based on *The Wizard of Oz*. No one has live music, let alone musical theater, at marketing events. Well, that is until in 2022. Some people created a crowdfunded musical called *Crypto: The Musical*.

We began doing live music because I'm a jazz saxophonist and our CEO thought it would be a cool outlet for me. After a few years, we realized that live music, an original theme song, and other forms of entertainment were part of our secret sauce. And while not everyone appreciates that part of our event, it's something we will keep doing. It's part of our DNA.

What can you combine to make your event unique?

#4: Consider your unique competitive advantage.

Do you know what makes your team unique? Have you ever made an inventory of the passions, skills, and interests of your staff to see what makes your people tick? Find out what lights them up. See if perhaps you have some hidden talents or secret advantages that can help you become totally different from any of your competitors.

I love flying on Southwest Airlines when possible. The biggest reason is I love to be surprised by the flight attendants. Sometimes it's an ordinary experience like every other airline, but often an attendant will break out into a song, rap, or comedy routine. Southwest encourages staff to use their passions and talents to improve the guest experience.

This isn't just about creating a talent show or finding those hidden skills. It's also about finding how the combined skills and passions of your team set you apart.

I'm currently part of a new church plant. We have fewer than 100 people involved, but there are thirteen professional counselors and four more in grad school to become licensed therapists. That is a high concentration of people in the helping industry. The church leadership has been asking, "What does this make possible?" We're already looking at ways to serve teachers who have been affected by stressors in education but who likely can't afford ongoing counseling.

Make a grid of all your skills and personalities. See what you discover.

> Asking "What does this make possible?" can be one of your most liberating (and challenging) questions.

#5: Ask what industry you are really in.

We alluded to this earlier, but it's worth making a unique point about this. In my case, I may think I'm in the events and education industry. The truth is, I'm in the entertainment industry. People come to events I lead to not only learn but also to have experiences they can't have at home. If I don't deliver on that promise, they will leave disappointed. At minimum, they won't return. At worst, they'll tell all their friends to stay away.

What about you? What industry are you in?

Let's say you are a dentist. Is your business to be a tooth cleaner, or are you a smile maker?

If you're a smile maker, who is your competition? Movies. Chuck E. Cheese. Disney. Comedians.

If those are your competitors, how will you run your business differently?

Bread Bite

You have the opportunity to create something unique by combining elements that already exist.

Question: What unique skills and attributes does your team have that can help you create one-of-a-kind experiences for your customers?

Exercise: Take one of the five principles in this chapter, and brainstorm ten ways to apply this to your next event experience. Here they are again:

1. Understand your competition
2. Look for inspiration in unexpected places
3. Combine the known to create the unknown
4. Consider your unique competitive advantage
5. Ask what industry you are really in

Chapter 15:

AMPLIFYING YOUR EVENT: MAKING IT SHAREABLE

I'll never forget the Secret Family Reunion I took to Italy with Haute in 2019. Not only was it the most epic reveal on our destination, I had to work really hard to go. It required a massive change of plans to rearrange my schedule and get a passport with only two weeks' notice. But the experiences we had together were unrivaled. From having a layover in Iceland where we saw the Northern Lights to having pasta in the shadow of the Leaning Tower of Pisa. From hunting for truffles to making pizza and pressing olives. From having dozens of memorable conversations to making lasting friendships. When I got home, I found myself posting about the event for several weeks. I couldn't help it. Nobody asked me to do it. I just had to share some of the lessons I learned and experiences we had.

Do you ever wonder if the decisions you're making as an event organizer impact sales? In many organizations, event planning is separate from marketing, so there can seem to be a disconnect.

I felt this way for many years until I had this revelation: **producing a great event is the best form of ongoing marketing**. A highly shareable event increases retention and FOMO.

Marketing 101

I'm not a marketer, but I've been working with marketers for decades. Not only have I worked for a marketing education company for a dozen years as of this writing, but I also worked for several others marketers throughout my career. Some things have rubbed off on me. Here are a few lessons I encourage you to apply to your events.

#1: Know your audience avatar. We discussed this in Chapter 11, but it's critical that you market the event to the right people. If you're talking about something your core audience doesn't care about, you'll need to find a way to appeal to those who do (or should) care. When you have a deep understanding of who your event is for, you can refine your messaging.

I spent seven years on the board of directors for Digital Wichita, an educational nonprofit in Wichita, KS. In 2022, we decided to focus on personal branding for our event. In our initial messaging, we were only appealing to entrepreneurs and business owners. We grew to understand that many employees care about their personal brands. We added some speakers who could address why employers care about personal branding and started to feature this. The impact on sales was immediate.

#2: Highlight what your audience cares about. If you know your audience intimately, you can talk about what they care about as opposed to what *you* think is important or cool. In fact, they might get scared if you talk about some of the changes you hope will happen to them. They do care about the outcomes, but the process might feel overwhelming.

Almost every year at Social Media Marketing World, we asked our audience before and after the conference what their priorities were for the conference. Even when we were discussing networking, the number-one priority was learning. In fact, nearly 80% of our attendees claim this as their top priority.

I know for a fact that what attendees talk about after the event is networking, relationships, and experiences. They'll remember a few learning tidbits, but what they cherish is the community. But we can't focus too much on that in marketing, except for the alumni. Our alumni messaging will appeal to the sense of "summer camp meets business conference." For all new prospects, we focus on learning opportunities. Do you know what your audience really cares about?

#3: Experiment constantly, and study the data. Before I started working with a marketer, I assumed that marketing was all about being hypercreative. It turns out that marketing is half creativity and half analytics. A good marketer is constantly experimenting to get the right message in front of the right audience with an offer that meets a real need. This requires ingenuity, persistence, and careful attention to the data.

When I helped plant a church in Hinsdale, Illinois, we sent flyers in the mail. It seemed counter intuitive since I always throw those away with the junk mail, but when we started seeing people show up and a few families joined the church as a result we decided to keep investing money in this tactic. It only took one or two families joining to pay for the campaign.

In marketing, you can't get too attached to your ideas. You might think it's brilliant, but if your customers don't care, it doesn't matter. Likewise, don't prejudge an idea. Just because it wouldn't work for you doesn't mean it won't work for your audience.

#4: Form strategic partnerships. Partnerships can be an excellent form of marketing. Whether through affiliate relationships, sponsor agreements, or formal marketing partnerships, you can dramatically increase the reach of your event by strategically partnering with others. Just be clear on what your arrangement is. I've seen that this is especially valuable when you're first getting started with your event. At a certain point, your strategic partners will lose interest, or you may find that they aren't driving the traffic to your event they once did. Honor your loyal partners, but also acknowledge when it's time to become independent.

#5: Attendee communication is a form of marketing. For your customers to get the most out of your event, they need information at the right time in the right place. When you provide this, your guests will relax and keep leaning into the experience you've designed. If they are confused or lost, they will spend more energy focused on logistics than the experience. That will lead to frustration and the potential of a negative experience (and review).

Ask your marketing team to help you design a strategic communication plan that gets attendees the information where they prefer to consume it in a timely manner. We've found that not everyone reads emails. Have a variety of means for getting the information. It can include a private website, a mobile app, social media, and even a printed guide. Err on the side of overcommunicating. Some people might get annoyed if they read everything you send, but most people will only see some of your messages and will be glad.

In 2022, some of our team attended several new events in the Web3 space. The communication to attendees at these events was sparse—one sent only one email and it was a mere three days before the event. As a result, people scrambled to understand what was happening. That felt very disorganized and disjointed.

Your guests will thank you for communicating clearly, and this will start to build the community before your event ever starts. And when people have a great experience they will start talking about your event.

Social Media 101

In Chapter 8, I discussed how social media can help build community at your event. It also serves a role in marketing your event to current and future customers. Here are a few additional tips:

#1: Choose your platform wisely. If you are hosting an event for aeronautical engineers or brain surgeons, TikTok probably isn't the best platform for you to focus on. Instead, figure out where your audience spends the majority of their time. To understand this, you can research statistics on current usage patterns. I'm not going to share any because they will be dated by the time you read this. Simply ask them. Perhaps upon registration or in a survey soon after registration, create a short survey that asks what social media platforms they use in addition to a few other strategic questions you might have.

#2: Use hashtags strategically. You can't copyright protect a hashtag, so make sure you research if anyone else is using the hashtag you plan to use. When finding a hashtag for Crypto Business Conference 2022, we assumed

#CBC22 would make sense. But it turns out that lots of events, churches, and communities use that hashtag. It's not necessarily a problem that someone else uses the same hashtag as you, but just make sure it's usage won't be peaking at the same time as your event.

Once you select your hashtag, make it known in all your communication. Ask your staff to consider changing their social handles to include the hashtag. This works especially well on Twitter.

For customer service issues at a larger event, I recommend having sub-hashtags. For instance, if your event hashtag is #ABCD2023, your customer service hashtag might be #ABCD2023help.

Be sure to have a team of people monitoring all your hashtags across any platform where your audience might be posting. Using a monitoring tool can make this much easier. Keep on the lookout for spam riders. These are people who watch for trending hashtags and then start posting all kinds of smut and spam using your hashtag to get extra eyeballs. You can sometimes report these posts, but remember that you don't "own" your event hashtag. It's borrowed for free.

#3: Create cool photo opportunities. Everyone's a photographer these days. You'll see people posing for pictures or taking selfies throughout your event. Give them reasons to take pictures. Make your graphics photoworthy. Create spots where people want to take a picture (e.g., photo booths). Perhaps even create a contest where people share pictures of your event using a specific hashtag.

If you have great content and fun people and experiences, you shouldn't have to work too hard to get people to share your event. But it doesn't hurt to reward the most active community members. We met Brian Fanzo, one of our future speakers at our first event because he was consistently the top tweeter. Turns out that his motto was true: "I talk fast and tweet faster." His handle is @iFanzo.

#4: Highlight posts. Get your social media team prepared to highlight and reshare top posts throughout the event. It's smart to have some form of social wall where you can curate those pictures and posts. People love to see themselves on the big screen.

#5: Monitor and moderate. Your social team has another important job besides creating and sharing fun content. You need them looking for problems and discontented guests. We've found that people prefer to get on social media to complain versus get up and find a staff member. One year, we had community members complaining about a guest who was stalking other attendees. They sent us a picture. We hunted him down until we could confront him. Turns out he didn't have a ticket, so it was easy to escort him out.

#6: Provide access to WiFi. If possible, provide free access to WiFi throughout your event, especially if you expect people to share their experience and it's not easy to access their data plans. Here's a caveat. WiFi services for thousands of people can become a six-figure expense—especially at a facility where there is an exclusive provider. As long as personal data plans work, you may find it better to let people fend for themselves. This is one of those costs that seems essential until you start counting. If your event attracts international guests, be sure to advise them on how to get WiFi or local cellular coverage if you aren't providing it.

#7: Stick to your 90-day plan. In Chapter 11, I introduced you to Erin Gargan King's 90-day social media plan. Be clear on your plan before, during, and after the event. An important lesson is to have teams of people who own different phases of your involvement. Your on-site team will be burned out after the event. Have different people ready to take over during this phase.

Something Shareable

"There's no long such a thing as an "offline" experience because every experience, no matter where it occurs, can be captured on the smartphone in your pocket and shared with the world in an instant."
—Dan Gingiss, *The Experience Maker*

In the last section, we discussed making it easy to share things on social media from your event. Now let's discuss creating moments that are shareworthy.

You could argue this whole book has been about creating those moments, but some memories are more personal and others aren't necessarily worth sharing. Here are some ideas:

#1: End your event in a spectacular fashion. Whether it's with an indoor fireworks show, a massive party on a cruise ship, or the world's largest autograph party, do something people will talk about and want to share with their friends. The more unexpected and unusual, the more likely they are to share it. If you can make it logical and personal, it will stick in their brains. If you can make it highly visual, it will get shared numerous times.

#2: Do something original. Lean in to your community and culture to create something truly original and unforgettable. I'll never forget the ATD (American Talent Development) event where a group created the world's largest drum circle. They taught us to play our parts and then brought us together. We formed a rhythm section. It was fun, but then they debriefed the experience, and we took away numerous lessons on the value of teamwork and listening.

At our event, we've written original songs, performed musical parodies, and hired a TikTok artist to create a live painting in the middle of the event. On several occasions, we've created a flash mob moment where dancers appeared out of nowhere to surprise and delight the audience.

#3: Invite your speakers and celebrities to key moments. If your audience is eager to meet your speakers, create moments where this can happen easily. Perhaps you have a bookstore with book signings, or you create autograph booths. You can strategically invite your speakers to show up in the registration area while your guests are arriving.

Remember how Disney gets a princess to show up to celebrate a little girl's birthday? What if you could get a speaker to show up to celebrate one of your guests?

Sharing is Caring

You've heard the cliché "sharing is caring?" Well, there's actually truth in it. Ultimately, people share with their friends and family things they enjoy and find valuable. Concern will drive them to tell others about important lessons and experiences they've had. It could be through social media or simply telling stories in everyday conversations.

Let's be honest for a moment. People are most likely to share positive and negative experiences, but not the neutral "meh" moments. As long as you maintain goodwill with your audience, they are far more likely to share the positive experiences. Just be sure to have a team watching for ways to turn the negative experiences into positive memories.

If you keep doing the right things, something powerful will start to happen. I'll never forget how after a few years of running our event I started hearing podcast interviews where speakers were telling the host that their career changed at Social Media Marketing World. In fact, I heard it dozens of times. I felt affirmed as I realized the experience we created allowed for those significant pivots, but it was also the first time where word-of-mouth marketing exceeded all of our paid marketing efforts.

If you create an unforgettable experience, your guests will share it, and it may even change their lives! And sometimes you'll hear about it!

Roger Wakefield came to our conference in 2018 after hearing a podcast interview with our CEO. His plumbing business was failing and he knew he needed help so he decided to attend our conference. Since it was a mere two weeks away, he paid full price. He arrived so early on the first day that the doors hadn't even opened, but he came back at 8 a.m. and spent the next few hours creating a plan for our three day event. During the event his wife called to say they had no more money and would need to shut the business down. He helped her find enough money to survive a couple of weeks and then got busy learning.

By the time the conference ended Roger decided to go all in on YouTube by creating three videos per week answering common plumbing questions. He quickly became the go-to YouTube channel for all plumbing-related questions. He was able to monetize his channel. He's now known as Roger Wakefield the Expert Plumber all over the internet. His online business is so successful that he sold the plumbing business in late 2021. And he attributes his success to our conference.

How do I know? He called me to tell me that our conference changed his life.

We don't always get to hear these stories, but when we do it fuels us to keep going.

Bread Bite

Amplifying your event not only lets you reach more people; it also deepens the memory for your attendees. Every time you retell a story it becomes more deeply imprinted in your brain.

Question: When you design your event, how can you plan for shareworthy moments? How will you implement that into your planning process.

Exercise: If event planning and operations is done separately from your marketing, get the two teams together to talk about how you can work together to create an integrated approach that feeds off each other. Look at your traditional marketing, your social media, and the opportunities within the event that might become candidates for amplification. Finally, think about how you might incorporate your alumni.

Section IV:

Conclusion

Chapter 16:

MIXING IT ALL TOGETHER

I'll never forget traveling to our conference in 2020. I had my saxophones with me in the waiting area, and a lady approached me to ask if I was a musician. I said yes, I'm a jazz saxophonist. It turns out she was an award-winning Native American musician. I happened to have my penny whistle with me, so she asked if she could play it. The entire waiting area went silent as we listened to her make incredible music. I didn't know that instrument could make such beautiful sounds.[19]

And then, when she found out I'm from Wichita, she broke into a song she wrong about Wichita. This all happened on the journey to the event and set the stage for what became an unforgettable event. It made me wonder what else is about to happen? My expectations were raised.

If people come to your event and have a great time but don't take home anything they learned, it's a failure. The event might as well have not happened, and there's no way to get back those days and dollars.

This chapter contains key lessons on how you can help attendees prepare for their experiences at your events.

Five Phases of a Successful Event Experience

Just as with going to a restaurant to enjoy a meal with artisan bread, there are five phases of the event experience that you can help your attendees prepare:

- 🎂 **Selecting the restaurant**—Finding the right city and venue can shape the whole experience.
- 🎂 **Traveling**– Sometimes the journey to your destination is half the fun.
- 🎂 **Dining**– This is the experience everyone expected, but it becomes memorable based on the details.
- 🎂 **Leaving the restaurant**– From the hostess to the valet, your departure experience is just as important as your arrival.
- 🎂 **Returning home**– If you go on a romantic date and have a great meal together but get in a spat on the drive home, the experience will be ruined. Same can happen for your event.

Let's explore each of these phases in detail as it relates to events.

Phase One: Selecting the Restaurant

When planning a special dinner, almost all of the work is done in the preparation phase. Selecting the restaurant, planning the menu, organizing the entertainment, and making a seating chart all make the event special. Likewise, I believe there are at least five things an event organizer can do preconference to help attendees have a memorable experience.

#1: Make travel planning easy. Travel can be one of the most intimidating parts of attending a conference. Here are some ideas of things you can do:

- 🎂 Share ideas on finding flights or transportation.
- 🎂 Get deals from airlines.
- 🎂 Have an official event hotel or block of hotels allowing attendees to stay close to the action where they can increase the likelihood of those

serendipitous conversations that can transform their experience from ordinary to truly memorable.

#2: Create a preparation plan. Many attendees need to prepare for physical demands that are beyond their normal experiences such as extended periods of standing on their feet and extensive walking. Think through your event. Identify what's different from how your attendees might normally function. How can you help them be better prepared? Preparing for our conference, I knew I needed to address the standing and walking issue, so I invited staff and volunteers to join me in a Fitbit challenge to get to 10,000 steps and more per day. We always have moleskin on hand for blisters and encourage attendees to bring comfy walking shoes that are already broken in. Comfort can be more important than fashion when you're standing for hours at a time.

#3: Plan the journey. If you planned a special dinner party, you would send an invitation with important details and a map. You can help your attendees plan by providing tools for determining their schedules. If you use a mobile app, give them access a few weeks in advance. They can plan their session attendance, social activities, and downtime. Advice from prior attendees makes it easy to know which sessions and activities would be best for them. One of the things we do is host a pre-event orientation webinar so new attendees can better plan for their experience.

#4: Give goal guidance. A good dinner host knows the goals and tastes of her audience. She would never knowingly serve foods that trigger allergies nor would she choose music that alienates her guests. She wants to create a welcoming environment to facilitate memorable conversations. Likewise, you should help your attendees get clear on their goals. You can be suggestive or more directive with this depending on the nature of your event. It's funny how sometimes we attend events and don't prepare adequately so we can maximize the time spent.

#5: Help them get to know fellow attendees. I'll never forget eating alone in a Swiss restaurant where I ordered fondue. I had just spent seven months in Kenya where we ate everything with our fingers, so I forgot that fondue was for dipping and tried to eat straight from the bowl. If I had been with a friend, I could have avoided that embarrassment. Did I mention I was sitting in the middle of the restaurant with all the locals chuckling at me?!

At conferences, most people want to experience it with other people even if they don't know anyone before arriving. For at least half of your audience, this may be the most stressful part of your event. Find ways to help attendees make friends before arriving. We have discovered that social media and the event mobile app are two great vehicles for this. Your situation may vary.

Phase Two: Traveling

Have you ever gone to dinner in a limousine? What about driving an hour or two to go to a special restaurant? That journey becomes part of the experience. In the same way, attendees who travel a few hours or even a full day (or two) count those experiences as part of the journey.

I see three parts of the traveling phase.

#1: Overcoming entropy. One of the hardest parts about travel is that it requires us to get out of our routines and comfort zone. While the forces that prevent change may not be as obvious, they can be just as powerful. As we discussed in Chapter 4, the forces working against attendees can be captured with the acronym DRIED: Dullness, Resistance, Isolation, Exhaustion, Distraction.

Dullness: The worst critique you can receive at your event is a collective yawn. Having people angrily leave is better than passive participation. A boring event leads to inoculation, which means you've protected your customers from the very change they need. So much money and time are wasted on events that lead to little change in performance or behavior. What will you do to make your event not just exciting but significant?

Resistance: In his book, *The War of Art*, Steven Pressfield describes the three forces of resistance facing all creative activities: fear, uncertainty, and doubt. These forces plus cynicism prevent us from leaning into the event experience and can, in fact, cause us to leave mentally and/or physically. How can you help your attendees know they belong? What can you do to diffuse their potential cynicism?

Isolation: One of the main reasons people attend conferences is to be around other people who share the same passions, interests, and questions.

But the very sense of isolation that drove them to your event can also prevent attendees from stepping into the conference experience. The more you can make it easy to meet people early in the event, the less likely this will be a negative force. We've found that focusing on having five meaningful interactions in the first twenty minutes upon arrival can have a dramatic effect on an attendee's experience the rest of the conference. Twenty minutes isn't magical, but it does remind us that it needs to happen early and authentically. How will you overcome the forces of isolation?

Exhaustion: Self-care is a buzzword these days, but it has a dramatic impact on the conference experience. If attendees arrive exhausted, dehydrated, undernourished, or sick, they will not engage and may even have a bad experience. We advise people to arrive early, especially if they are coming from overseas. Getting enough sleep and water can dramatically improve the disposition of attendees so they can engage with the content, speakers, sponsors, and fellow attendees. What can your team do to help attendees manage their exhaustion?

Distractions: Social media is a great tool. Yet in the midst of a conference, it can be the very thing that prevents attendees from fully engaging in the event. As the leader of a social media marketing event, I obviously want people to use social media, but it also thrills me to hear what Ann Handley, Chief Content Officer for MarketingProfs, said to her social media followers following our event. I'll paraphrase it here: "Sorry for being absent the last three days. I was at a social media conference and became so immersed in the conversations and experiences that I forgot to post."

Distractions can also be in the form of problems at work or home, health concerns, or any number of things. How can you help people leave these distractions and prepare for a fully immersive experience at your event?

#2: Trusting the babysitter. If you're going on a romantic date, you need a babysitter who you feel can competently take care of your kids. Otherwise, one of you will be constantly checking in on the kids and not enjoy the date. For event attendees, some extra actions are required to be able to leave work and home issues behind. One recommendation will feel counterintuitive but will pay massive dividends. Pete Vargas, founder of Advance Your Reach, introduced me to this idea. At the start of your event, invite attendees to send a video or a text to a boss and/or a loved one thanking them for their support and encouragement while they attend this conference so they can learn.

#3: The arrival. Have you ever been to a restaurant where they recognize you and call you by name as soon as you walk in? Neither had I until I went to a Ritz-Carlton. Everyone knew that I was Mr. Mershon (side note: my dad never did show up, so I was a bit confused). For event attendees, the arrival experience is a moment of great danger and joy.

Why danger? This is a first-impression moment. If your staff members are disinterested, distracted, or disorganized, it will make the attendee feel unimportant and maybe even frustrated. Conversely, if it feels like you've been waiting for your attendee to arrive, she will feel special and know that you care even if something doesn't go perfectly. Greet your attendees by name. Look her in the eye. Find unexpected ways to help.

For most attendees, the arrival is a culmination of months of planning. There's anticipation and excitement but also fear. No one likes that moment when they don't know what to do. You feel very exposed and uncertain. This is the opportunity for your team to step in and "make their day." It can be as simple as finding ways to engage your new attendees in conversation, offering to help take her to her first session, showing her the way to find some food, or just bringing her a cup of coffee or water.

Phase Three: Dining

Events and restaurant experiences have a lot in common, but here are three insights from restaurants that might help your next event be even more impactful.

#1: Stay focused on your guest experience. Both of my daughters have been successful as restaurant servers and bartenders, but not all of their peers have the same success. The difference is their focus on the customer experience. They are constantly watching and regularly checking in. They focus on elevating the experience and their tips reflect that attention to detail.

At events, it's easy to become enamored by the latest gadgets and technologies. When you go to a conference and see someone experimenting with holographic images, LED screens, or virtual reality it's easy to get FOMO.

Event producer Richard Steinau, VP with Worldstage, says that 60% of the requests he receives are frivolous and don't help the event accomplish its mission. In other words, they are a distraction from helping attendees enjoying their meal and they are a waste of money. Why do attendees come to your event? Make sure to ask that at every step and stay focused. What a tragedy to go to a restaurant and forget to eat the famous dessert! If your attendee returns to the office and only talks about how great the parties were and how cool the technology was but has nothing to offer that will make her company better, it's highly unlikely she'll be approved to attend your event next year.

#2: Prepare for the unexpected. When you're baking bread, any number of things can go wrong. That's why smart event organizers have contingency plans for all known problems and train their staff for them. The unfortunate blessing of fire alarms going off during our staff training forced us to evacuate the building for 30 minutes. We learned firsthand how it really works instead of just reciting the rules. And it was not exactly the same as we had been told. While I don't advise manufacturing a fire drill, it's smart to rehearse your responses to this and anything else you know can go wrong.

#3: Monitor your energy levels. Restaurant servers who don't take regular breaks put themselves in danger. I vividly remember the time I watched my daughter almost pass out because she hadn't been given a break in eight hours and she was famished. Unfortunately, too many event producers forget to do this, too. We work twenty-hour days, forget to eat and hydrate, over caffeinate, and fail to take time to breathe. No wonder we sometimes become irritable and even bite the heads of our team members. Self-care is vital to your ability to create the experience you desire. The saying is, "Love your neighbor as yourself." If you don't love yourself, then you can't love your neighbor very well.

#4: Provide real sustenance. If given a choice, do you prefer a fast-food restaurant or a sit-down restaurant for the nutritional value? That's really not a question. Our bodies prefer highly nutritious meals just as our brain desires valuable content. If you serve up snackable content, the results will be a quick hit but no lasting change. Instead, focus on creating a well-balanced menu of content experiences and then leave them time to digest their food. Chalene Johnson, author of *Push*, builds time into her agenda at the Marketing Impact

Academy for students to start implementing what they learn. She doesn't want to keep them up late at night only to go home without any tangible takeaways and actions. Are you giving your audience time to reflect upon and start trying things they are learning?

Phase Four: Departure

Can you imagine a bride who hasn't planned her getaway moment? That doesn't happen, but you can catch the groom off guard most of the time! It's like he didn't know people throw bird seed or might put confetti in his car—or doesn't think his groomsmen might try to follow him.[20]

Well, great event organizers need to be more like a bride than a groom. They know the event doesn't end until people get back home. They understand that events will not become epic or transformational unless the story lives beyond the few days of the event. Here are some tips to help bring better closure to your next event:

#1: Storing and categorizing your findings. When I spoke with the baker, Josh Allen, he talked about his studious approach to finding the right recipe for his clients. He documented everything he did and carefully watched his customer's response to each sample until he found the right recipe. Jesse Cole meets nightly with his Show Caller to review the game and document their learnings. This requires foresight. As an event organizer, you know that many attendees won't think about this without prompting. They may think about some of it, but they probably haven't thought through how they will capture and store their ideas so they can follow up on them later. I encourage you to find ways to make this easy.

One idea here is to do what Jeff Hurt, CEO of Velvet Chainsaw, does. At the conclusion of an event, he will lead attendees through a series of exercises where they will take their top three learnings, and turn those into stories, pictures, and elevator pitches. He invites participants to share these learnings in various ways to stimulate the brain and body to cement these lessons into their long-term memory. But then he goes further and invites attendees to make a covenant to follow up in 21 days with one fellow attendee to see how their implementation progress is going.

Another idea is what Michael Hyatt does at some of his events. He invites participants to create a 90-day action plan for implementing their biggest takeaways. And he helps them create this plan before they leave and even provides follow-up reminders after they leave.

How can you help your attendees capture, store, and take action on their key takeaways?

#2: Saying goodbye. Wedding guests throw rice. Dinner hosts hand out gifts. The Savannah Bananas end the night singing "Stand By Me." Your event attendees need a way to say one last goodbye to their new friends and anticipate the next gathering. They need a sense of closure.

True confession. I inadvertently planned our event for several years in a way that prevented this. Let me explain. After our closing keynote, I invited our volunteers and staff on stage to take a group picture. That sounds like a smart idea, right? Well, here's the unintended consequence: not one of us was around to say goodbye to our speakers and attendees because we were on the stage. As a result, the conclusion was anticlimactic for many attendees. We changed that in 2019, and while we don't have hard data that proves it was better, there were certainly a lot more smiles and conversations.

#3: Return home. When you've had a life-altering experience, it's easy to go back home and return to old patterns. Entropy is a hard force to overcome. But it doesn't have to be that way.

Authors Kerry Patterson, Joseph Grenny, David Maxfield, Ron McMillan, and Al Switzler share a six-fold model of change in their book *Change Anything*. It can be helpful for guiding attendees toward the lasting change they may want to make. They identified six sources of influence that can work for or against you in the intended change.

Source #1 is personal motivation. How badly do you want this change? How important is it for you to make this change? What's at stake if you fail to change?

Source #2 is personal ability. Normally change requires you to do something you currently can't do. It requires you to deliberately learn a new skill set. This requires discipline, resources, and often a coach or a course.

Source #3 is turning accomplices into friends. People in our lives can either help or hinder us from making change. The key is finding those who will support, encourage, coach, and challenge us to change.

Source #4 is hard conversations. Talk with these allies about your goals and reasons for the change. Those who resist or oppose your change need to have less influence over you. That may require creating temporary or permanent distance.

Source #5 is structural motivation. This has to do with incentives. What incentives for change can you create that will keep you motivated to keep changing? A dieter might reward themselves with a cheat meal after two weeks of successfully following the plan. If taking a course, perhaps there's a celebration upon completing a semester or a module. The goal is to get some quick wins and keep the incentives small and achievable. Too many lofty goals are forgotten for lack of momentum.

Source #6 is structural ability. This is creating systems and changes in our physical practical world that facilitate change. An alcoholic trying to recover would never survive in a house with a fully stocked bar. A messy office might create too much mental distraction for the creative writer seeking to finish her book. Encourage people to make changes to their worlds that will enhance the likelihood of change.

Phase Five: Returning Home

Returning home after an epic dinner or vacation can feel like a whirlwind. Most of us don't prepare for it. I remember listening to Emily P. Freeman, author of *The Next Right Thing*, reflect on this. She commented that it's a lot like astronauts not planning for their reentry. They would never do that—it would be disastrous. But most people give little thought to what they will do when they get back home. As a result, little changes. The same is true for event attendees. Here are three things you can do to help with their return home:

#1: Prepare for the questions. Those who experience transformation at a conference will be asked many questions back at the office or the house. Preparing answers to those questions can help shape the narrative and increase the likelihood of change. I encourage people to have an elevator pitch of a 30-second answer that is meant to whet the appetite of the curious and satisfy everyone else. For the curious person who wants to hear more, I advise having a two-minute response that can lead to a much deeper conversation if they remain curious. Stories make for great elevator pitches. Everyone loves a great story, but here's the problem: without your guidance, most of your attendees will focus on the exciting or the unimportant stories.

Here's an example. A few years ago, a homeless man was taking a spit bath in the women's restroom at our event. One of our staff members walked in on him, and the story quickly spread about "the naked man in the women's bathroom." It became a legend among our staff. But what if that story was what people told their bosses and spouses about our event? Or what if they only talked about how great the parties were but not about the transformational takeaways? Your guidance can help attendees turn these conversations into a positive first step toward the lasting change they desire and increase the likelihood they will return to your next event.

#2: Take time to decompress. Wise attendees will add a day to their trip or plan a personal day to rest and sort through their learnings before returning to normal life. Encourage your attendees to get buy-in toward this approach with their bosses and families. If the conference was worth attending, it should be worth an extra day to make sure the learnings are captured and incorporated into a plan.

#3: Make time to study and implement your findings. What a tragedy if all the loaves of bread were thrown into a closet with junk. Many of our modern comforts and technologies wouldn't exist if "bakers" hadn't taken the time to learn from their experiments. The same is true in business. Businesses and careers won't change if attendees don't make plans for how they will continue to study and implement. We encourage attendees to schedule time for listening to recordings and to form masterminds or cohorts where they can continue to discuss and share ideas.

Having a follow-up plan can be the difference between a wasted investment and a 10x investment. Help your attendees find the best solution for their situation.

Bread Bite

Doesn't it make sense to help your attendees take adequate time to prepare for all five stages of their event experience? Start by creating a simple plan for each of the five stages. Which stage looks like it needs the most help? Focus on improving that for your next event.

Last Bite

This book has led you through a process for helping you create your recipe for making memorable event experiences. As you strategize your events, take time to think through each ingredient and phase. There's no such thing as a perfect event, but you can create a great event and make yours one that people remember for many years. In short, you can make it **unforgettable**!

I challenge you to go take your first step today.

Here's to your success.

Appendices

Appendix A:

NEXT STEPS

Congratulations for making it this far. You're well on your way toward creating unforgettable experiences.

You may be wondering what you can do next. Here are a few options:

1. Get the Bonus materials

🍞 Go to philmershon.com/unforgettable/bonus to get some extra interviews and resources to help you on your unforgettable journey. You'll need the password: "breadbites" to log in. Here are some of the things you'll find:

- A recommended list of books, websites, articles, and podcasts to help your keep learning.
- Detailed discussions on some of the more complicated steps.
- Interviews with some of the experts mentioned in the book where we explore further the ideas introduced in the book.
- A discussion of virtual and hybrid events.

- An outline of how this translates into churches and nonprofit ministries.

2. Speaking

⚓ If you'd like me to speak for your company, event, or podcast, fill out the form at philmershon.com/speaking and I'll be in contact to discuss opportunities.

3. Follow me. Here are the best ways to follow my writing and speaking:

⚓ Subscribe at philmershon.com/subscribe to get regular updates and to be notified when new articles and podcast episodes release.

⚓ Listen to the Unforgettable Experience podcast on your favorite podcast platform.

⚓ Social media. Follow me here:

- LinkedIn: linkedin.com/in/philmershon/
- Facebook: facebook.com/phil.mershon
- Twitter: twitter.com/phil_mershon
- Instagram: instagram.com/phil_mershon

Appendix B:

DRIED TO TAST-E

Negative Views

	Belief	Feeling	Thinking	Relating	Action	GOAL
Dullness	I don't need this.	I feel misunderstood.	I've heard this before.	These aren't my people.	I'd rather take a nap.	Transformative
Resistance	This is below me.	I feel guarded or agitated.	These people don't know what they're talking about.	Nobody wants to be with me.	I feel so over-whelmed I'm going to leave.	Accepting
Isolation	I don't have much to offer.	I feel inferior (or superior) so won't bother to engage.	I'm too intro-verted, and social settings make me anxious.	It's more comfortable to sit alone.	I will withdraw and stay to myself.	Together
Exhaustion	I need to do every-thing.	I'm afraid to miss out on something (FOMO).	I can sleep later, so bring on the coffee.	Meeting new people wears me out.	Events always make me sit too long.	Stimulating
Distraction	I don't want to miss out on what's happening online.	I feel confused by all the competing messages.	I've got too many thoughts and can't slow down to orga-nize them.	I can't focus because I might be missing another con-versation.	I'm constantly bombarded by messages pulling me away from the event.	Engaging

Positive Views

	Belief	Feeling	Thinking	Relating	Action	GOAL
Positive Views						
Dullness	This is for me.	I feel seen.	I am intrigued.	I belong.	I want to improve.	Transformative
Resistance	I'm right where I need to be.	I feel accepted and affirmed.	I am challenged to think differently.	There are many people here worth meeting.	I will slow down to extract as much value as I can.	Accepting
Isolation	I believe one conversation could change my life.	I am seeking serendipity.	Most of these people feel like I do.	Every person here has a story worth hearing.	I will take the initiative to start a few conversations each day.	Together
Exhaustion	The best things happen when I'm well rested.	I'm eager to discover the unexpected.	If I set boundaries and make good choices, I can accomplish more in less time.	Meeting new people opens me to new possibilities.	I know how to manage my energy and will come ready.	Stimulating
Distraction	Being fully present will open the door to the biggest changes.	I feel empowered to create my own journey and focus.	I can create focus and make time for deep thinking.	I can stay fully focused on each person while I'm with them.	I will turn off all notifications.	Engaging

ABOUT THE AUTHOR

Phil Mershon is director of experience for Social Media Examiner; for over 12 years he has created amazing customer experiences at events like Social Media Marketing World and the Social Media Success Summit. Throughout his 30+ year career, Phil has been creating memorable experiences for businesses like Koch Industries, as well as non-profits, schools, and churches. He is also a jazz saxophonist, pickleball enthusiast, and a songwriter. Phil lives in Wichita, Kansas with his wife, Audrey, and their three adult children and their standard poodle, Millie the Therapy Dog.

ABOUT THE ILLUSTRATOR

Born in 1961 in Queens, NY, Lisa Rothstein was told by Depression-Era parents that she'd be "out on the street selling pencils" should she pursue a career as a cartoonist. This led to a job as a copywriter at the ad agency Young & Rubicam New York after graduation from Brown University in 1982. She quietly pursued her cartooning on the side, taking night classes from New Yorker cartoonists as she worked with brands like IBM (recruiting *Hagar the Horrible* creator Chris Browne for one long-running award-winning print campaign). Today Lisa freelances as a live sketchnote artist, brand strategist, and a cartoonist whose work has appeared in *The New Yorker*, several bestselling books, and marketing campaigns. Lisa lives in San Diego, California. She enjoys using pencils, but so far has not been seen selling any.

Learn more at www.drawingoutyourgenius.com

INTRODUCING REMEMBRANDT

Learn more: philmershon.com/remembrandt

ENDNOTES

1   Dokimazo means to test or examine in Greek. I wish they left this in their name to remind us all to keep on experimenting

2   Go here to see Mike Rayburn perform Green Eggs and Ham in Led Zeppelin's style: https: //www.youtube.com/watch? v=yY5D8uRDV54

3   https: //www.cdc.gov/sleep/about_sleep/drowsy_driving.html

4   https: //www.healthline.com/nutrition/coffee-nap#effectiveness

5   https: //www.studyfinds.org/dancing-boosts-mood/

6   Firth, J., Torous, J., Stubbs, B., Firth, J. A., Steiner, G. Z., Smith, L., Gleeson, J., Vancampfort, D., Armitage, C. J., & Sarris, J. (2019). The "online brain": how the Internet may be changing our cognition. *World Psychiatry*, *18*(2), 119-129. https://doi.org/10.1002/wps.20617

7   Entrepreneur (2018). Distractions Are Hurting You More Than You Realize: Here's Why [online]. Available here. [Accessed Feb 2021.]

8   Will, D., Bao, D. and Jerome, D. (2018). 'The Extra Hour,' London: Virgin Books.

9   https://convene.com/catalyst/meeting-event-planning/event-planning-most-stressful-jobs/

10 For more details, go to: https://www.storycraftlab.com/experience-profiles

11 *I will occasionally not name an event as my goal is not to disparage any event.

12 https://www.wsj.com/articles/SB10001424127887323932604579050990 895301888

13 Two books to help with this are: *Intentional Event Design: Our Professional Opportunity* by Tahira Endean and *What Color Is Your Event?: The Industry Resource on How to Think and Plan Creatively* by Dianne Budion Devitt

14 https://www.linkedin.com/pulse/showing-up-powerful-ly-10-tips-event-organizers-speakers-phil-mershon/

15 For instance: https://www.ncbi.nlm.nih.gov/pmc/articles/PMC3049465/

16 For more details, see the book *What Color is Your Event?* by Diane Budion.

17 https://www.socialtables.com/blog/meeting-event-design/types-of-seating-arrangements/

18 See *Everything's Coming Up Profits: The Golden Age of Industrial Musicals* by Steve Young if you want to learn about it.

19 I tried to look up the lady's name. I think she went by WindWalker, but I can't find a recording of the Wichita song she sang.

20 Because I had followed one of my groomsmen after his wedding and had a little too much fun at the expense of another one, I privately asked my new brother-in-law, a Deputy Sheriff, to provide us a police escort away from the wedding. It worked!

A free ebook edition is available with the purchase of this book.

To claim your free ebook edition:

1. Visit MorganJamesBOGO.com
2. Sign your name CLEARLY in the space
3. Complete the form and submit a photo of the entire copyright page
4. You or your friend can download the ebook to your preferred device

Print & Digital Together Forever.

Snap a photo   Free ebook   Read anywhere

Printed in the USA
CPSIA information can be obtained
at www.ICGtesting.com
JSHW081917040823
45985JS00001B/2

9 781636 981017